The hands-on guide t

Invaluable information for sch
providers and further educatio ...ges in 2009/10

Nick Linford
Special Adviser on Funding and
Performance
Edexcel
London, UK

This book is as balanced, practical and accurate as I could make it.
Ideas for improvements are always welcome via email to:
nick.linford@fundingguide.co.uk

For further information and updates visit www.fundingguide.co.uk

The hands-on guide to post-16 funding
First published October 2009
Reprinted 2010

Text © Edexcel Limited

Edexcel Limited
190 High Holborn
London WC1V 7BH, UK

Book orders can be placed via the website.
To order via the website, please go to: www.fundingguide.co.uk/

ISBN 978-1-84690-735-7

Linford, N (Nick)
The hands-on guide to post-16 funding
Illustrations by Nick Linford, London, UK
Typesetting and page layout by The Publishing Centre, Oxford, UK
Printed in Great Britain by Henry Ling Ltd., at the Dorset Press, Dorchester, Dorset

We are grateful to the following for their permission to reproduce copyright material:

Page 19: table from *Presentation to AoC Finance Directors' Conference*, LSC (June 2009)
Page 19: graph from *Our Statement of Priorities*, LSC (November 2007)
Page 22: extract from QCA website (June 2009)
Page 57: extract from *LSC Grant Letter 2006/07*, DfES (October 2005)
Page 73: extract from *Funding Guidance 2009/10*, Update v4.0, LSC (July 2009)
Page 74: extract from *FLT: 14–19 Delivery Guidance for 2009/10*, LSC (August 2009)
Page 74: diagram from *Foundation Learning Tier: Interim Guidance*, LSC (May 2009)
Page 77, 78, 79, 81: diagrams from *The Diploma: an overview of the qualification*, QCA, Version 3 (2008)
Page 104: extract from *Unit Funding Trials 2008/09 – 2009/10*, LSC (December 2008)
Page 110: extract from *£100m Response to Redundancy Pre-employment training programme guidance for providers*, LSC (April 2009)
Page 112: diagram from *Skills provision for those reaching six months' unemployed delivery plan v3.0*, LSC (May 2009)
Page 113: extract from *Funding Guidance 2009/10 v4.0*, LSC (July 2009)
Page 115: diagram from *Flexible New Deal Preferred Bidder Presentation*, DWP (June 2009)
Page 120: extract and table from *Statement of Priorities*, LSC (November 2008)
Page 123: extract from *Funding Guidance 2009/10*, LSC (July 2009)
Page 145: table from *Framework for Excellence: Unified Post-16 Performance Assessment*, LSC (July 2009)

Every effort has been made to trace the copyright holders and we apologise in advance for any unintentional omissions. We would be pleased to insert the appropriate acknowledgment in any subsequent edition of this publication.

Content overview

Detailed Contents

Glossary of abbreviations

AFI: assumed fee income

ALN: additional learning needs

ALS: additional learning support

ALSN: additional learning and support needs

ASL: adult safeguarded learning

ASN: additional social needs

BIS: Department for Business, Innovation and Skills

CSR: comprehensive spending review

DCSF: Department for Children Schools and Families

DIUS: Department for Innovation, Universities and Skills

E2E: Entry to Employment

EFL: English as a Foreign Language

EfW: ESOL for Work

ESOL: English for Speakers of Other Languages

FE: further education

FEFC: Further Education and Funding Council

FfE: framework for excellence

FL: Foundation Learning

GLH: guided learning hour

HE: higher education

HEFCE: Higher Education Funding Council for England

HEI: higher education institution

IELTS: International English Language Testing System

ILR: individualised learner record

LAD: Learning Aim Database

LLDD: learners with learning difficulties and/or disabilities

LSC: Learning and Skills Council

LSF: learner support funding

MLP: minimum levels of performance

NDAQ: National Database of Accredited Qualifications

NDPB: non-departmental public bodies

NEET: not in education, employment or training

NFR: national funding rate

NQF: National Qualifications Framework

NVQ: National Vocational Qualification

OLASS: Offender Learning and Skills Service

PaMS: planning and modelling system

PF: provider factor

PSA: public service agreement

QAA: Quality Assurance Agency

QCA: Qualifications and Curriculum Authority

QCDA: Qualifications and Curriculum Development Agency

QCF: Qualifications and Credit Framework

SfBN: Skills for Business Network

SfJ: Skills for Jobs

SLN: standard learner number

SSoA: summary statement of activity

TtG: Train to Gain

UKVQRP: UK Vocational Qualification Reform Programme

WBL: work-based learning

Author's introduction

This second edition (2009/10) of *The hands-on guide to post-16 funding* is a reference guide for anyone with an interest in LSC learner- and employer-responsive funding. It covers the national demand-led funding formula, as applied in school sixth forms, further education colleges (16–18 and adult), and other training providers. However, *this guide cannot be the authoritative source of LSC information on funding*, as that remains with the authors of it, namely the LSC (*see page 15*).

This guide is a complementary tool that I hope helps to summarise the workings and implications of LSC funding rates, eligibility and methodology. It should be useful for everyone working in the post-16 learning and skills sector. It contains ten chapters, and the topics covered within each are spread across two pages. This serves two purposes. Firstly, it should make it easier for you to find information (without the need for an index). Secondly, two pages per topic means I have had a volume constraint, which, given the complexity of topic, is probably welcome.

The first edition of *The hands-on guide to post-16 funding* was published in September 2008 when the demand-led funding methodology was first introduced. This edition has been rewritten for 2009/10 to take account of changes to the rates and guidance, which I have summarised on page 24. I have included new sections on the Qualifications and Curriculum Framework (QCF), Foundation Learning (FL), functional skills, the Learning Aim Database, and new chapters for Apprenticeships, Train to Gain, and the pre-employment programmes being delivered by colleges and training providers in response to the economic recession.

A lot has happened since the publication of the last book. The impact of the recession and restrictions on funding has led to a number of late changes, some of which delayed publication. Plus, whilst writing this book I got married, bought a house and left Lewisham College to join the Edexcel Policy and Curriculum team.

Finally, I would like to acknowledge and thank a number of people. At Edexcel: Siân Owen for all her determination, hard work and being the driving force behind the book; Bob Osborne for commissioning a new edition; Trevor Luker and Steve Besley for supporting both me and the project, Andrew Crimp for design ideas, and finally Liam Wynne and his team for all their marketing support. Alex Cook at the LSC for commenting on the draft and putting up with all my questions, and all the other commentators on page 8 and 9 for supporting the project. Finally, I would like to take this opportunity to thank my new wife Sarah and my parents, Denis and Sandra Linford, for their uncompromising love and encouragement.

Comments from across the sector

I am proud to be able to sponsor and publish this updated and revised edition of *The hands-on guide to post-16 funding*, particularly as since the publication of the first edition, we have been delighted to welcome the author, Nick Linford, on to the staff at Edexcel. Together with writing this new funding guide, he will also be running planning and funding training events for the post-16 sector, starting with a series of Train to Gain and Apprenticeship funding masterclasses (see www.planningandfunding.co.uk). We appreciate that an effective understanding of funding can have a huge impact on the successful running of a centre, and on the range of provision you can offer your learners. We strive to constantly innovate to provide a better service, and we are pleased to be able to offer you this additional support, particularly given the challenging economic times we are all currently working in.

Trevor Luker, UK Education Commercial Director, Edexcel

With the severe funding pressures facing the learning and skills sector in England and the anticipated cuts, it has never been more important to not only be wise spenders but to be even wiser earners and understand how courses are funded. This guide will help the FE sector navigate their way through the emerging complexity of funding, at this time of swift change. It includes useful worked examples and diagrams and should be used as a resource to support the learning and skills sector drive for continuous self-improvement and capacity building. We are lucky – and glad – to have it.

Dame Ruth Silver, Chair, Learning and Skills Improvement Service (LSIS), previously Principal of Lewisham College

The contract year 2009/10 will bring some difficult challenges for providers. In particular the changes to the funding agencies and to the responsibilities for 16–18 commissioning. This funding guide will be essential reading for all learning providers that need to understand the detail of the complex funding system so that they can optimise the delivery of their programmes to learners and employers.

Graham Hoyle, Chief Executive, Association of Learning Providers (ALP)

The newly created College of Haringey, Enfield and North East London welcomes this clear and accessible guide to LSC funding. We pride ourselves on designing and delivering innovative learning opportunities across a wide range of educational and workplace settings, and to do that we need to be able to navigate our way through what can often be a complex set of funding rules. This guide is a resource which will enable us to understand exactly how resources are made available from the LSC, in order to provide the best possible experience for both learners and employers. The new chapter on pre-employment programmes is a particularly welcome addition as colleges continue to play a key role in supporting the economic recovery.

Paul Head, Principal & Chief Executive, The College of Haringey, Enfield and North East London

Local authorities will be taking on responsibility for commissioning and funding 16-19 education and training in April 2010. I wholeheartedly recommend this book to all those local authority colleagues who will be working in the 16–19 area, as it provides a clear, concise and straightforward exposition of a complex area, suitable both for senior managers who require a general overview, and for operational managers working with providers, who need to understand the detail. Understanding the funding mechanisms, and the underpinning incentives and disciplines, is an essential starting point to operating an intelligent commissioning system.

John Freeman CBE, Director, React Programme

Whilst this funding guide is not written or endorsed by the LSC, it may prove a valuable resource for those wanting to know how the LSC funding methodology works in practice, the funding changes for 2009/10, and Edexcel's view of the current plans for funding in 2010/11. Nick is a well-respected member of the FE sector and has an excellent understanding of the funding system and how it works on the ground.

Alex Cook, Senior Funding Policy Implementation Manager, Learning and Skills Council (LSC)

The context

The Government is 'determined to build a world-class skills base for a competitive future, ensuring that all young people and adults have the skills they need for employment and progression, and supporting stronger, more productive and more competitive businesses'. (*LSC Grant Letter 2009–10*, DCSF and DIUS (November 2008))

14–19-year-olds

The 14–19 reform programme dominates the education landscape for young learners as we move towards raising the minimum education and training age, an entitlement to access new curriculum and qualifications from 2013, and a common performance management system across all post-16 providers. The demand-led formula in this guide is not used to fund 14- and 15-year-olds, but the Government's long-term ambition is that it will be extended to cover the whole 14–19 phase.

Apprenticeships

The Government want apprenticeships to be a mainstream option for 16–18-year-old learners, with the ambition that, by 2019/20, one in five young people will have started an apprenticeship before the end of the academic year in which they reach their 18th birthday (from one in 15 at present). In April 2009 the National Apprenticeships Service (NAS) was launched (*see page 116*).

Adult skills

The Government remains committed to the 2020 ambition for world-class skills, but recognises that hitting the associated targets will become more challenging as businesses and individuals respond to the economic downturn. However, the focus in 2009/10 is still very much on a demand-led system which aligns funding with the Government's key priorities and targets (*see page 13*).

Pre-employment programmes

In response to the economic recession, a series of new funding streams specifically designed to support adults in gaining employment have been launched. Many providers will become involved in these types of programmes for the first time, so this guide has a chapter dedicated to these programmes (*see page 107*).

Machinery of Government (MoG) changes

After the passing of the Apprenticeships, Skills, Children and Learning Bill, the Learning and Skills Council (LSC) will be wound down. It will be replaced from April 2010 by the Young People's Learning Agency (YPLA) and the Skills Funding Agency (SFA). In addition, local authorities will take on the LSC's role of commissioning and funding all 16–18 learner-responsive provision in colleges (*see page 148*).

The rest of this chapter explores where the funding for education and training comes from and what it funds. It also includes a section on the developing Qualifications and Credit Framework (QCF) as well as the main changes to the demand-led funding methodology for 2009/10.

Government funding

In June 2007 the Department for Education and Skills (DfES) was replaced by two new departments: the Department for Children, Schools and Families (DCSF) aims to 'make England the best place in the world for children and young people to grow up' and oversees education and funding for those up to the age of 18; the Department for Innovation, Universities and Skills (DIUS) aims to 'apply both knowledge and skills to create an innovative and competitive economy' and oversees education and funding for those beyond the age of 18. In June 2009 DIUS merged with the Department for Business, Enterprise and Regulatory Reform (BERR) to become the Department for Business, Innovation and Skills (BIS). Both DCSF and BIS receive funding from the Treasury, and pass some of this on to the Learning and Skills Council (LSC) to fund providers for the delivery of education and training in England.

The 2009–10 projected flow of government funding

Sources: *Budget 2009 Report*, HM Treasury (April 2009) and *LSC Grant Letter 2009–10*, DCSF and DIUS (November 2008)

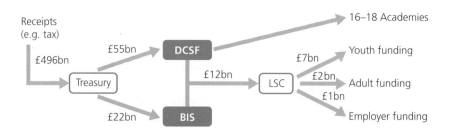

Both Government departments have given the LSC a participation budget for 2009–10 which is 5% higher than the previous year.

LSC budget for participation, including specialist provision

Source: *LSC Grant Letter 2009–10*, DCSF and DIUS (November 2008)

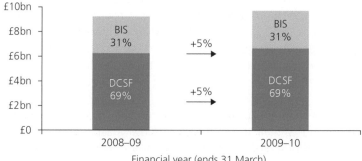

However, this real-terms growth in funding comes with important strings attached, known as Public Service Agreement (PSA) targets. There are 30 PSAs that cover all government departments, and will to a great extent dictate what is, and what is not, an LSC funding priority until 2011.

Three of the 30 PSAs relate to post-16 education and training, and each PSA contains a number of measurable national targets.

DCSF is the lead department responsible for:

1. Raising the educational achievement of all young people by:

   - increasing the proportion of young people achieving Level 2 at age 19 from 71% in 2005/06 to 82% in 2010/11;

   - increasing the proportion of young people achieving Level 3 at age 19 from 47% in 2005/06 to 54% in 2010/11.

2. Increasing the number of young people on the path to success by:

   - reducing from 10% in 2004 the number of 16–18-year-olds not in education, employment or training (NEET) by two percentage points.

BIS is the lead department responsible for:

3. Improving the skills of the population by:

   - ensuring 597,000 adults achieve their first Level 1 (or above) literacy or ESOL qualification, and 390,000 achieve a first Entry Level 3 (or above) numeracy qualification from 2008/09 to 2010/11;

   - increasing the proportion of working-age adults qualified to at least full Level 2 from 70% in 2006 to 79% by 2011;

   - increasing the proportion of working-age adults qualified to at least full Level 3 from 49% in 2006 to 56% by 2011;

   - ensuring 130,000 apprentices complete the full apprenticeship framework in 2010/11 (a rise from 98,000 in 2005/06);

   - increasing the proportion of working-age adults qualified to Level 4 and above from 30% in 2006 to 34% in 2011 and to 36% in 2014;

   - increasing participation in higher education, of those aged 18–30, from 43% in 2005/06 towards 50% by 2010.

Funding is heavily prioritised for qualifications that can deliver these PSA targets. Conversely, funding will continue to reduce for provision that does not. It is also worth noting that QCF interim definitions for full Level 2 and full Level 3 have been introduced (*see page 23*).

Learning and Skills Council

The Learning and Skills Council (LSC) is the largest non-departmental public body (NDPB), which, in 2001, took over the roles of the former Further Education Funding Council and the Training and Enterprise Councils. The LSC is responsible for planning and funding education and training in England for nearly everyone over the age of 15, other than those in universities. For the 2009–10 financial period, the LSC has been allocated more than £12 billion by the Government to spend as follows:

LSC Budget 2009–10

Source: *LSC Grant Letter 2009–10*, DCSF and DIUS (November 2008)

1. learning participation (82%)

2. learner support and development (9%)

3. capital grants (7%)

4. LSC administration (2%)

The LSC has a head office in Coventry, and until April 2010 will continue to plan and fund delivery from nine regional offices and through partnership teams which cover broadly the same areas as the approximately 150 local authorities in England. Find out more by visiting www.lsc.gov.uk

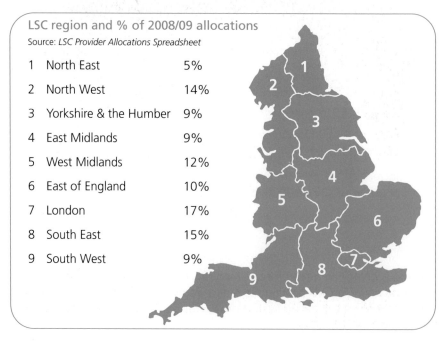

LSC region and % of 2008/09 allocations

Source: *LSC Provider Allocations Spreadsheet*

1	North East	5%
2	North West	14%
3	Yorkshire & the Humber	9%
4	East Midlands	9%
5	West Midlands	12%
6	East of England	10%
7	London	17%
8	South East	15%
9	South West	9%

LSC funding guidance for 2009/10

In addition to planning and funding delivery, the LSC are responsible for devising and maintaining the funding methodology, formula and relative qualification rates for all the funding models. The demand-led funding methodology was introduced in 2008/09, and rather than produce a new set of guidance documents for 2009/10, the LSC have published an update. The update is 'a technical reference document, and should be used in conjunction with the various LSC funding guidance booklets issued for 2008/09'. Therefore, the definitive 2009/10 funding guidance can be found in the following eight documents. There is also a separate 2009/10 guidance document for school sixth forms.

1. *2008/09 Funding Rates*
2. *2008/09 Funding Formula*
3. *2008/09 Principles, Rules and Regulations*
4. *2008/09 ILR Claims and Audit Returns*
5. *2008/09 ILR Funding Compliance Advice and Audit Guidance*
6. *2008/09 Learner Eligibility Guidance*
7. *Addendum to LSC Funding Guidance 2008/09*
8. *LSC Funding Guidance 2009/10 – Update*

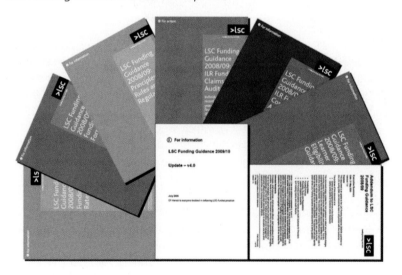

Amendments to the LSC funding guidance

There may be in-year changes or clarifications to the funding guidance, so providers should regularly check the LSC website for updates.

After the LSC

The LSC will cease to exist from April 2010. Responsibility for the funding methodology will then reside with two new agencies, the Young People's Learning Agency (YPLA) and the adult Skills Funding Agency (SFA). To find out more about the changes see page 149.

16–18 learner-responsive funding

The Department for Children, Schools and Families (DCSF) fund 16–18-year-old learners. The 16–18 learner-responsive budget for the 2009–10 financial year will be nearly £6bn. This includes funding for academies, although they do not receive their funding via the LSC.

Planned 16–18 learner-responsive funding: England 2009–10
Source: *LSC Grant Letter 2009–10* (November 2008) (excluding specialist provision)

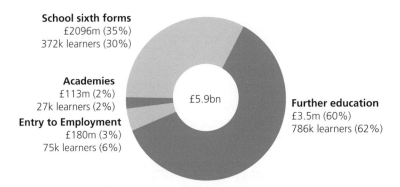

School sixth forms
£2096m (35%)
372k learners (30%)

Academies
£113m (2%)
27k learners (2%)

Entry to Employment
£180m (3%)
75k learners (6%)

£5.9bn

Further education
£3.5m (60%)
786k learners (62%)

Individual provider allocations for the 2009/10 academic year were set based on these budgets in March 2009. However, many providers felt that their allocations were insufficient for the anticipated demand from learners. In June 2009 the LSC announced that they had secured an additional £655m from the DCSF (£251m for 2009–10 and £404m for 20010–11), which would fund a further 54.5k 16–18-year-old learner-responsive places in the 2009/10 academic year. Of these additional places, 22k was awarded through a competitive process in which providers of all types submitted business cases.

The funding methodology used for school sixth forms, including that for the success factor (*see page 42*), is very similar but not identical to that used for colleges, owing to different data collection regimes. All learner-responsive funded providers are subject to the same demand-led funding formula (*see page 27*). However, the national funding rate for schools is 3% higher than that for colleges (*see page 30*).

This edition of *The hands-on guide to post-16 funding* has a chapter dedicated to school funding (*see page 59*) and another for 16–18 college funding, including Entry to Employment (*see page 71*).

> **Note**
>
> Apprenticeship provision for 16–18-year-olds is also funded by the DCSF, but this sits within the employer-responsive funding model (*see page 20*) alongside Train to Gain.

The range of LSC-funded providers

A range of provider types deliver LSC-funded 16–18 learner-responsive provision, as shown in the diagrams below.

2008/09 16–18 learner-responsive allocations
Source: *LSC Allocations Spreadsheet*

1. School sixth forms (34%)

2. FE colleges excluding sixth forms (49%)

3. Sixth form colleges (13%)

4. Other providers (4%)

2008/09 16–18 learner-responsive average allocations
Source: *LSC Allocations Spreadsheet*

16–18 funding beyond March 2010

In April 2010 the LSC will cease to exist, and 16–18 funding will be the responsibility of a new agency, the Young People's Learning Agency (YPLA). The YPLA will pass funding on to local authorities, who will pay the individual providers. Sixth form academies use the same demand-led formula but receive funding directly from the DCSF. The plan is that funding for academies will become the responsibility of the YPLA.

National Commissioning Framework (NCF)

The NCF will set out the core systems for planning, commissioning, procuring and funding 16–18-year-olds, 19–25 learners with a learning difficulty and/or disability (LLDD), and young people in custody. It will be operational in time to agree 2010/11 allocations. Providers can participate in the consultation phase and find out more at http://www.dcsf.gov.uk/14-19

Adult learner-responsive funding

Adult learner-responsive (ALR) funding is for adults (aged 19 and over) who, in the main, attend further education colleges. However, there are a number of other provider types, such as local authorities and higher education institutions that also receive ALR funding (*see pages 93–105 for more on ALR*).

The national ALR budget has reduced in recent years, as funding has been redirected to flag-ship programmes like Train to Gain (*see page 127*). Also, ALR funding has shifted away from provision which does not contribute to the PSA targets (*see page 13*). 2009–10 has been no exception, with overall funding for ALR reducing by 2%, within which non-priority 'developmental learning' has been cut by 39%.

Planned adult learner-responsive funding: England 2009–10
Source: *LSC Grant Letter 2009/10*, DCSF and DIUS (November 2008)

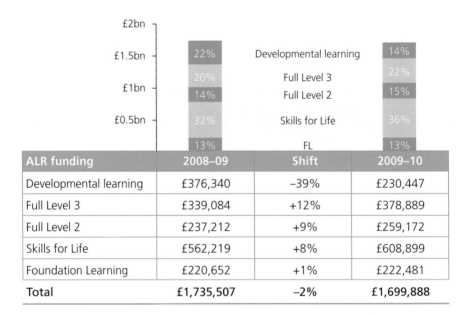

ALR funding	2008–09	Shift	2009–10
Developmental learning	£376,340	−39%	£230,447
Full Level 3	£339,084	+12%	£378,889
Full Level 2	£237,212	+9%	£259,172
Skills for Life	£562,219	+8%	£608,899
Foundation Learning	£220,652	+1%	£222,481
Total	£1,735,507	−2%	£1,699,888

A new flexible approach below Level 2

Colleges and providers will still be expected to deliver Skills for Life priorities, but in response to the recession will have the flexibility within their 2009/10 allocations, across pre-Level 2, to respond to local circumstances. However, this flexibility does not come with additional funding, and the majority of providers (66%) had reduced ALR allocations (*see table on next page*). The type of provision and qualifications on offer at colleges is likely to remain, to a great extent, dictated by what contributes to PSA targets.

2009/10 Adult learner-responsive allocations

Source: *Presentation to AoC Finance Directors' Conference*, LSC (June 2009)

% Change	Number of providers	% of total
−10%	97	19%
−5% to −10%	131	26%
−5% to 0%	105	21%
0% to +5%	96	19%
+5% to +10%	27	5%
>10%	43	9%
Total (excl. 33 new providers)	499	100%

Skills Accounts and only funding priority provision

The long term ambition is that by 2015 all adult learner-responsive model funding will be via skills accounts (currently being piloted). This includes a timetable as part of the UK Vocational Qualification Reform Programme (UKVQRP) and introduction of the Qualifications and Credit Framework (QCF) (*see page 22*) to fund only those qualifications that are classed as a high priority. The LSC stated within their investment strategy for 2009–10 that 'skills accounts are an integral part of the offer to individuals, together with the adult advancement and careers service, and will over time become the single way in which individual adults access public funding to support their learning'.

Projected shift in adult learner-responsive model funding

Source: *Our Statement of Priorities*, LSC (November 2007)

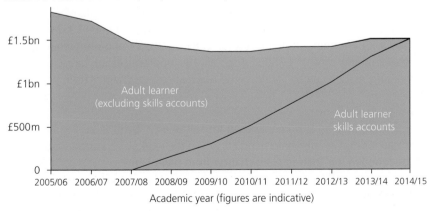

Academic year (figures are indicative)

ALR funding beyond March 2010

By April 2010 the LSC will cease to exist, and adult funding will be the responsibility of a new agency, the Skills Funding Agency (SFA).

Employer-responsive funding

The employer-responsive funding model consists of apprenticeships and Train to Gain provision, both of which are funded from a version of the LSC's national demand-led funding formula (see page 27). Apprenticeships are funded for both young and adult learners, so the budget comes from both government departments.

2009–10 employer-responsive budgets (financial year ending March 2010)
Source: LSC Grant Letter 2009/10, DCSF and DIUS (November 2008)

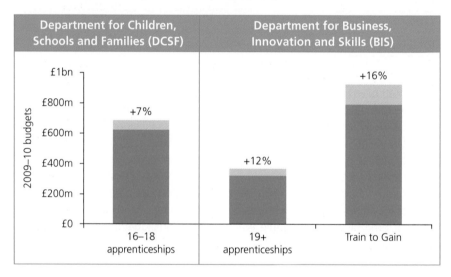

Apprenticeships
Apprenticeships aged 16–18 have a 2009/10 national funding rate of £2920 and are fully funded. The 19+ apprenticeship budget is shared between 19–24-year-old learners with a national funding rate of £2817 and 25+ apprenticeships with a national funding rate of £2535. Also, all 19+ apprenticeships are co-funded. Further information can be found in the Apprenticeships chapter from page 116.

Train to Gain
Train to Gain funding is primarily used for full Level 2, Level 3, and Skills for Life qualifications that are delivered to adults within the workplace. Further information can be found in the Train to Gain chapter from page 126.

Note
Provider allocations are for the academic year ending July. However, the LSC budget is for the financial year ending in March. When funding is tight this can cause problems for monthly payments (see page 134).

Key differences between the employer, 16–18 and adult learner-responsive models.

Employer-responsive model	16–18 and adult learner-responsive models
Monthly instalments in which payments are calculated for each enrolment from actual delivery.	Payments monthly on agreed profile not actual delivery (with some reconciliation for adults).
Payments based on actual weighting for each enrolment.	Payments based on an historical provider factor calculated from 2007/08 delivery (see page 32).
Achievement funding 25% for Train to Gain and 25% (excluding key skills and technical certificate) for apprenticeships.	Retention and achievement funding accounted for by the success factor within the provider factor (see page 42).
Withdrawal may impact on funding as payment based on monthly instalments.	Funding not reduced if learner is withdrawn after minimum attendance period (see page 54).
Funding claims submitted every fourth working day of the month.	Funding claims submitted five times for a year (minimum).
Fee element (funding deducted) is weighted by the provider factor and the employer contributes.	Fee element is not weighted by the provider factor and learner pays the fee (see page 52).
Ten programme weightings.	Seven programme weightings (see page 34).
Limited number of eligible qualifications.	Wide variety of eligible qualifications.
All funding rates listed as SLNs.	Some rates unlisted, and listed rates are SLN glh (see page 28).
The learner's workplace defines area costs uplift. Train to Gain ineligible for disadvantage uplift.	The provider's main site defines area costs uplift (see page 38) and learners eligible for disadavantage uplift (see page 36).
No per learner cap on funding.	Annual per learner cap of 1.75 SLN (see page 29).
Monthly performance monitoring, with quarterly success rate reports using an ER success rate methodology for overall and timely achievements.	Less frequent monitoring and annual success rate reports using an LR success rate methodology (which does not include timely).

Qualifications and Credit Framework

The Qualifications and Credit Framework (QCF) is being introduced as part of the UK Vocational Qualification Reform Programme (UKVQRP). The QCF is now live and by December 2010 it will have fully replaced the National Qualifications Framework. This means that all vocational qualifications accredited into the NQF will not have an accredited end date beyond 31 December 2010, and any new accreditations from 1 January 2010 will have to be within the QCF.

The QCF: a new **framework** for **recognising and accrediting qualifications** in England and Northern Ireland. The framework is at the heart of a major reform of the vocational qualifications system designed to make the whole system **simpler to understand and use** and **more inclusive**. The intention is to make both the system and the qualifications offered, far **more relevant** to the **needs of employers** and more **flexible and accessible for learners**.

Source: *QCA website* (June 2009)

'Simpler to understand and use'

Every qualification within the QCF has the potential to be an Award, a Certificate or a Diploma at nine different levels. Each qualification will contain one or more units, and each unit will consist of one or more credits.

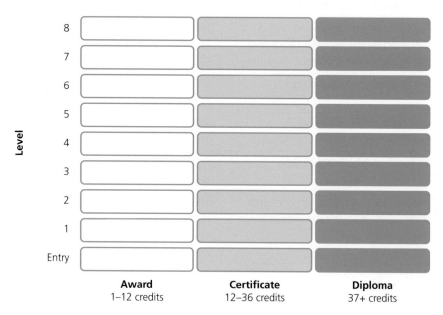

Level			
8			
7			
6			
5			
4			
3			
2			
1			
Entry			
	Award 1–12 credits	**Certificate** 12–36 credits	**Diploma** 37+ credits

One credit represents 10 hours of learning time. Learning time is not the same as guided learning hours (glh) because it includes homework, assessment and preparation time. This is important since the LSC only set qualification funding rates based on glh (*see page 28*).

'More relevant to the needs of employers'

As part of the implementation of the QCF and vocational qualification reform, LSC will be using the Sector Qualification Strategy Action Plans (SQS APs) to inform funding eligibility decisions and SSCs will advise the LSC on which key qualifications should be funded.

'More flexible and accessible for learners'

Learners can in theory enrol on individual units and either progress to the next unit with the same provider or take their unit with them to a new provider. This is known as Credit Accumulation and Transfer (CAT), although there are strict Rules of Combination (RoC) which specify which units need to be achieved to be awarded the relevant Award, Certificate or Diploma. Quite how flexible and accessible the QCF becomes will in practice depend not only on the policies of the individual providers, but which qualifications and units are made available for funding.

Note

Credits can only be awarded through the completion of a whole unit. Also, in many cases credits from a lower level can contribute to an Award, Certificate or Diploma at a higher level.

New QCF interim definitions of full Level 2 and 3

In November 2008 an interim definition of 13 credits or more for a full Level 2 was announced, and in June 2009 an interim definition of between 25 and 70 credits for a full Level 3 was set. However, the Sector Skills Councils, Sector Bodies and Standard Setting Bodies are able to vary these thresholds up or down when determining which qualifications are full. The introduction of these new interim definitions is significant because the adult entitlement to fee remission, and the availability of qualifications for programmes like Train to Gain, require qualifications to be full.

Funding QCF qualifications and units

Qualifications and stand-alone units in the QCF are funded using SLNs and the demand-led funding formula (see page 27). For example:

BTEC WorkSkills (Level 2)	Credits	SLN glh	SLN
Award	3	25	0.056
Certificate	13	120	0.267
Diploma	37	360	0.8

The double funding nightmare

The problem with CAT is that there is a high risk of double funding. Providers will need to 'discount' the funding for QCF credits that learners have already gained via field A51a in the individualised learner record (ILR). This will be very bureaucratic and could be a significant audit risk.

Main changes in 2009/10

The table below contains a list of the main changes to funding for 2009/10. However, a few additional changes are still being considered, so the LSC website should be monitored for any in-year updates.

Change type	Change description	Find out more on page
National funding rates	National funding rates have been increased to take account of inflation.	30
Train to Gain programme weightings	Programme weighting K (1.5) (excluding Skills for Life) has been replaced by C (1.3) and J (1.25) has been replaced by L (1.2). Skills for Life K (1.5) has been replaced by F (1.4).	35 and 129
Higher and lower Train to Gain rates	The higher and lower Train to Gain SLN rates have been scrapped. All Train to Gain qualifications now have one rate.	129
Fee element	The fee element has increased from 42.5% in 2008/09 to 47.5% in 2009/10.	52
Area uplift for Cambridgeshire	Cambridgeshire has been added to the area costs list, with an uplift of 1.02.	38
FL funded by E2E weekly payments	As a transition measure in 2009/10, learners on FL personalised learning programmes can be funded using the weekly funding methodology for E2E.	74
Some qualifications not fundable	The LSC have published a list of qualifications which are not eligible for funding new starts in 2009/10.	15
Qualification rate changes	The LSC have changed the SLN values for more than 160 qualifications. Some SLNs have gone up, others have come down. Some listed rates have become unlisted and some unlisted rates have become listed. The Learning Aim Database contains the rates for the relevant academic year.	138 and 140
School changes	There are a number of key changes.	61

Change type	Change description	Find out more on page
Rate for 25+ apprenticeships	All new 25+ apprenticeships starting from 1 August 2009 will be funded at 90% of the 19–24 rate.	122
New definitions of full Level 2 and 3	Interim full Level 2 and 3 definitions for QCF qualifications will mean the range of fundable Train to Gain provision is likely to expand.	22 and 129
Changes to additional learning support	The first £5500 of higher-level claims (claims over £5500 per learner) will no longer be included within the lower-level budget.	44
Adult entitlements	The Learning and Skills Act 2000 has been amended so that in 2009/10 there are legal entitlements for eligible adults not to be charged tuition fees for specified qualifications. See www.lsc.gov.uk/adultentitlement	18
Adult learner-responsive reconciliation rules	The reconciliation tolerances for 2008/09 were changed during 2008/09. In 2009/10 they will remain as originally published for 2008/09. For example, the final tolerance for clawback in 2009/10 will be 3%.	94
E2E rates	At the end of August 2008 the LSC announced SLN rate changes for E2E in 2009/10.	88

The following change is still being considered for 2009/10, and may be confirmed in an update to the funding guidance.

In-year adjustments to 16–18 funding allocations	The LSC funding guidance states that 'for 2009/10 we are working with representatives of the sector to develop proposals, to ministers, for a system whereby schools and colleges who underachieve on recruitment targets return some of the funds so that these funds can be allocated to providers who have over-recruited'.

The formula

The national demand-led funding formula was introduced in 2008/09 and remains largely unchanged for 2009/10. Every enrolment within the 16–18 and adult learner-responsive funding model uses this formula:

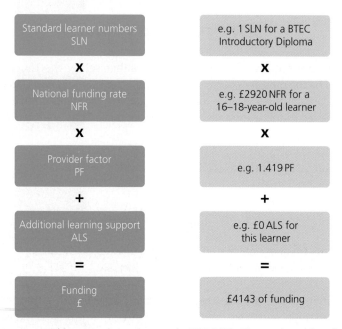

SLNs are generated by actual enrolments in 2009/10. The national funding rate is set by the LSC. The 'historical' provider factor contains elements which are calculated based on delivery in 2007/08.

This demand-led funding formula is also used to set provider allocations, as shown on page 46 and in the example below:

3000 SLN × £2920 NFR × 1.419 PF + £1m ALS = £13.4m allocation

Once this allocation is set the provider will only need to focus on generating 3000 SLNs to achieve the allocation as the national funding rate and provider factor is fixed before the start of the year.

A version of the demand-led formula is also used for employer-responsive funding (Train to Gain and apprenticeships) as it contains SLNs, a national funding rate and some of the provider factor elements applied in-year.

The demand-led funding formula was introduced in 2008/09 to simplify the formula that it replaced. Yet it is more complex than it at first appears as it must take account of provider, course and learner variables.

The following chapter covers each of the formula elements in detail.

Standard learner numbers

The standard learner number (SLN) is a measure of the volume of activity associated with the learning and is applied as the first element within the funding formula:

$$\text{SLN} \times \text{NFR} \times \text{PF} + \text{ALS} = \text{Funding}$$

Every enrolment has an SLN value, which is either set by the LSC (listed), or determined by the provider course size (unlisted). The Learning Aim Database (*see page 138*) contains the SLN value for every fundable qualification with a listed SLN value. However, in the learner-responsive model these SLNs are listed as guided learning hours (glh) called SLN glh.

To convert an SLN glh into an SLN it is always divided by 450.

$$\frac{\text{SLN glh}}{450} = \text{SLN}$$

If the learning aim does not have an SLN glh it is unlisted, so the actual glh recorded by the provider is divided by 450 to determine the SLN.

Guided learning hours are the hours of learning activity with a tutor or trainer. Therefore, SLN glh and SLNs are a measure of size, which is considered a key determinant of relative cost and therefore funding. SLNs are assigned to an academic year based on the start and end dates, and enrolments are added together to create a learner level SLN.

Unlisted SLNs

Unlisted SLNs describe those enrolments for which the LSC have not listed an SLN value, as a common size has not been identified. In this case every glh the provider delivers is worth 0.00222r SLN since glh is divided by 450 to derive the SLN value. This straight line divisor relationship between size and funding is important as it removes any incentive to increase efficiency by altering the course size.

Unlisted SLNs are primarily found in the adult learner-responsive model. In some cases a qualification can be both unlisted and listed.

Qualification	Funding	Duration	SLN (type)
Adult numeracy	Learner-responsive	90glh	0.2 (unlisted)
Adult numeracy	Learner-responsive	180glh	0.4 (unlisted)
Adult numeracy	Train to Gain	90glh	0.193 (listed)
Adult numeracy	Train to Gain	180glh	0.193 (listed)

Listed SLNs

The majority of learner-responsive qualifications have a listed SLN glh rate, and in the employer-responsive model all SLN values are listed (which are expressed as SLNs, so do not need to be divided by 450).

The table below is a first year A-level programme for a learner in the 16–18 model. All the SLN values are listed, so if the provider recorded and delivered different durations this would not alter the SLN values or the funding. The reference to 'daytime' is important as A-levels and GCSEs have a lower rate when taught in the evening (see page 62).

Sep '08 – Jul '09 daytime delivery	SLN glh	SLN
AS Economics	150	0.333
AS History	150	0.333
AS Politics	150	0.333
AS English	150	0.333
AS General Studies	36	0.08
Key skills in numeracy	36	0.08
Entitlement (including tutorial)	114	0.253
Total per learner	**786**	**1.747**

The SLN cap

The 'typical' programme above was the basis on which the LSC set an annual 1.75 SLN cap for all learners. Any additional enrolments would reduce the SLN value of all the enrolments such that the total does not exceed 1.75 SLN per year. In other words, the maximum amount of funding a learner can earn in one year is set at 1.75 SLN.

Note

The LSC set SLN glh values either based on awarding body recommended glh or their own analysis of actual delivery. Every year they review SLN values and some listed rates rise or fall and some become unlisted or listed. These changes should be monitored, but ultimately the actual glh remains a decision for the provider.

SLN as a currency

The SLN is not the same as any other volume measure. It is not the number of learners, and unlike full-time equivalences (FTEs) you can exceed 1 SLN per learner (see page 56). It may help to think of SLNs as a new currency from the Bank of the LSC. The national funding rate then coverts the currency into pounds and the provider factor acts as the provider exchange rate.

National funding rates

The national funding rate (NFR) converts the SLNs into an unweighted funding value within the demand-led funding formula:

$$SLN \times \textbf{NFR} \times PF + ALS = Funding$$

In 2009/10 there are five different national funding rates, across seven types of funding within the three funding models.

Funding Type	Funding Model	09/10 Funding Rate
School sixth forms	16–18 learner-responsive	£3007
16–18 colleges	16–18 learner-responsive	£2920
Adult colleges	Adult learner-responsive	£2817
16–18 apprenticeships	Employer-responsive	£2920
19–24 apprenticeships	Employer-responsive	£2817
25+ apprenticeships	Employer-responsive	£2535*
Train to Gain	Employer-responsive	£2901

* The actual rate used by the LSC is £2817, but this is discounted by 10% (*see page 122*).

The SLN value is multiplied by the relevant national funding rate to calculate the unweighted funding (before the provider factor and fee elements are applied to generate the actual funding).

Examples of unweighted learner-responsive funding

Provider	Qualification	SLN glh	SLN	NFR	Unweighted funding
School	GCSE	100	0.222	£3007	£668
16–18 college	AS level	150	0.333	£2920	£1002
Adult college	Access to HE	520	1.155	£2817	£3255

Examples of unweighted employer-responsive funding

Provider	Qualification	SLN	NFR	Unweighted funding
16–18 apprenticeship	Key skill	0.08	£2920	£233
Train to Gain	NVQ level 3	0.644	£2901	£1868

Inflation and affordability

The national funding rates are published each year, and change to take account of inflation and affordability.

Shift from 2008/09 to 2009/10 national funding rate

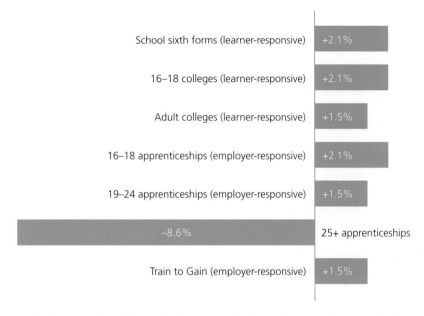

School sixth forms (learner-responsive)	+2.1%
16–18 colleges (learner-responsive)	+2.1%
Adult colleges (learner-responsive)	+1.5%
16–18 apprenticeships (employer-responsive)	+2.1%
19–24 apprenticeships (employer-responsive)	+1.5%
−8.6% 25+ apprenticeships	
Train to Gain (employer-responsive)	+1.5%

The introduction of a national funding rate (which replaced individual qualification rates in 2008/09) makes it relatively easy for the LSC to alter funding values for a particular funding type. Generally this would be upwards to take account of inflation. However, the national funding rates can also be reduced as a means to purchasing more places without increasing the level of resource.

For example, in June 2008 the LSC announced that the 2009/10 Train to Gain national funding rate would only be increasing to £2901 and not to the originally published figure of £2987. At the same time it was also announced that the funding rate for apprenticeship learners over the age of 24 would be reduced by 10% to £2535 from the originally published figure of £2817 (page 122 describes how this 10% reduction is applied).

Note

Some learner-responsive providers may have been set a transitional rate by the LSC in 2008/09 which could be higher or lower than the national rate. The LSC use transitional rates where they believe that the demand-led funding formula, all other things being equal, has created a significant winner or loser. Only a small number of school sixth forms have been given a transitional rate for 2009/10 (*see page 61*).

The provider factor

The provider factor is designed to take account of the relative costs associated with the course, location of delivery, certain groups of learners and quality. It is a weighting which sits within the learner-responsive funding model formula, for every enrolment and allocation.

$$\text{SLN} \times \text{NFR} \times \textbf{PF} + \text{ALS} = \text{Funding}$$

Only the learner-responsive funding model uses the provider factor in 2009/10 and a separate figure is calculated by the LSC for 16–18 and adult provision based on delivery in 2007/08. It is thus an historical average which is being applied within the learner-responsive funding formula.

The provider factor is calculated by multiplying a number of elements together, as seen in the diagram below:

		16–18	Adult
Programme weighting	See page 34	e.g. 1.246	e.g. 1.312
X		**X**	**X**
Disadvantage uplift	See page 36	e.g 1.081	e.g 1.072
X		**X**	**X**
Area costs uplift	See page 38	e.g. 1.200	e.g. 1.200
X		**X**	**X**
Short-programme modifier	See page 40	e.g. 1.001	e.g. 1.013
X		**X**	**X**
Success factor	See page 42	e.g. 0.877	e.g. 0.891
=		**=**	**=**
Provider factor		e.g. 1.419 PF	e.g. 1.523 PF

This calculation is made by the LSC every year, which means that while the provider factor remains unchanged during the year, it can change significantly from year to year.

Note

Actual delivery in 2008/09 will determine the provider factor in 2010/11 and delivery in 2009/10 will determine the provider factor in 2011/12. Therefore, although the provider factor does not change in-year, the five elements within it are being calculated for future use. It is therefore important to understand these elements in some detail.

Provider factor element	Brief summary of purpose and function
Programme weighting	Programme weightings recognise that some courses are more costly to deliver than others. There are ten weightings across the funding types ranging from 0% (1) to 92% (1.92). They are assigned to the learning aim within the Learning Aim Database (see page 138).
Disadvantage uplift	The disadvantage uplift recognises the additional costs incurred by providers in attracting, retaining and supporting disadvantaged learners (mainly based on where they live). This uplift is assigned at the learner level, and ranges from 0% (1) to 32% (1.32).
Area costs uplift	The area costs uplift takes account of relatively high costs of delivery within the South East of England. It ranges from 0% (1) to 20% (1.2).
Short-programme modifier	This uplift recognises slightly higher set-up costs for short courses below 225 funded hours. The shorter the programme the higher the uplift. $$\text{Short-programme modifier} = 1 + \left(0.3 \times 1 - \left(\frac{\text{Annual SLN}}{0.5}\right)\right)$$
Success factor	The success factor reduces funding by a half for learners who do not achieve their learning outcome. $$\text{Success factor} = 50\% + \frac{\text{Success rate}}{2}$$

These elements are likely to be of increasing interest to both school sixth forms and colleges because the provider factor is being used for the second time in 2009/10, having been updated after use in 2008/09 allocations. What might look like a small change to a provider factor can have a significant impact on the amount of funding that is allocated. Therefore, in this edition of the hands-on guide I have included detailed chapters for each of the five provider factor elements (see pages 34–43).

Employer-responsive provision
An historical provider factor is not used to generate funding for Train to Gain or apprenticeships. However, some of the provider factor elements are used. The apprenticeship funding formula uses the disadvantage uplift and both the apprenticeship and Train to Gain formulas includes the area costs uplift and programme weighting elements.

Programme weighting

The programme weighting is the first element within the learner-responsive provider factor.

$$PW \times DU \times ACU \times SPM \times SF = \text{provider factor}$$

The 2009/10 programme weighting is calculated separately for 16–18 and adult learner-responsive provider factors, and is a weighted average from actual delivery in 2007/08. Programme weightings recognise that some programmes are more costly to deliver than others.

A programme weighting is assigned to every learning aim for each of the relevant funding models. The learning aim is the eight digit code representing the course and providers can determine the programme weighting by using the Learning Aim Database (*see page 138*). Once a learning aim has been used within the enrolment data the LSC funding software references the Learning Aim Database and the correct weighting is applied.

Learner-responsive programme weightings

In 2009/10 the 16–18 and adult learner-responsive model will have the same seven weightings that were used in 2008/09. Each weighting is also assigned a letter.

Letter	Weighting	Example qualification
A	1 (none)	NVQ in Business and Administration
B	1.12	NVQ in Health and Social Care
C	1.3	NVQ in Beauty Therapy
D	1.6	NVQ in Construction Operations
E	1.72	NVQ in Agriculture Management
F	1.4	Basic skills specific (e.g. Level 1 Numeracy)
G	1.92	Particular qualifications in the agriculture and horticulture sector

In most cases the provider does not need to determine the programme weighting since the LSC have assigned it to the qualification. However, some courses (such as those which are non-accredited) require the provider to use the correct weighting letter as the last digit of a generic learning aim (*see page 138*). Generally the most reliable method for assigning the correct weighting in these cases is to use the Learning Aim Database to find the programme weighting for a similar course.

Employer-responsive programme weightings

The programme weighting is also used within the employer-responsive funding formula for both Train to Gain and apprenticeships.

$$\text{SLN} \times \textbf{PW} \times \text{ACU} = \text{Train to Gain funding}$$

$$\text{SLN} \times \textbf{PW} \times \text{DU} \times \text{ACU} = \text{apprenticeship funding}$$

In the employer-responsive model the programme weighting is not based on delivery in 2007/08, it is applied in-year to generate the funding for each individual enrolment in 2009/10.

Train to Gain programme weightings

The Train to Gain weightings have changed for 2009/10 and in general those weighted as K (1.5) in 2008/09 will be weighted as C (1.3) and those weighted as J (1.25) in 2008/09 will be weighted as L (1.2).

Letter	Weighting	Example qualification
A	1 (none)	NVQ in Business and Administration
L	1.2	NVQ in Health and Social Care
C	1.3	NVQ in Construction Operations
F	1.4	Basic skills specific (e.g. Level 1 Numeracy)

Apprenticeship programme weightings

The apprenticeship programme weightings remain unchanged in 2009/10.

Letter	Weighting	Example qualification
A	1 (none)	NVQ in Business and Administration
J	1.25	NVQ in Health and Social Care
K	1.5	NVQ in Construction Operations
A to G	1 to 1.92	The technical certificate weighting is taken from learner-responsive list

Note

The programme weightings have arguably become over-complicated, as for the first time in 2009/10 the same qualification could have three programme weightings (see the NVQ in Construction Operations example in each table above). Providers should always use the Learning Aim Database to determine the right weighting for the relevant funding type.

Disadvantage uplift

The disadvantage uplift is one of the elements within the learner-responsive provider factor.

$$PW \times \mathbf{DU} \times ACU \times SPM \times SF = \text{provider factor}$$

The 2009/10 disadvantage uplift is calculated separately for 16–18 and adult learner-responsive provider factors, and is based on delivery in 2007/08.

The purpose of the disadvantage uplift is to give certain learners a funding enhancement, which reflects their relative disadvantage and the expected additional costs incurred by providers in attracting, retaining and supporting such learners. In most cases the disadvantage uplift is based on the home postcode of the learner, which means it is applied at learner level to all enrolments. However, there are a number of other categories, and the provider should select the category with the highest eligible uplift.

Disadvantage uplift based on where the learner lives

This measure of deprivation is based on the home postcode of the learner. The LSC use the Index of Multiple Deprivation (IMD) 2004 (an index widely used by government) to rank deprivation for every super-output area (SOA) and related postcode in the country.

Basis for IMD 2004 deprivation ranking

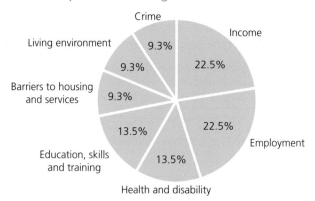

The SOAs (and their related postcodes) that are ranked in the 27% most deprived areas are allocated a disadvantage uplift between 8% (1.08) and 32% (1.32). Learners living in postcodes outside the top 27% receive no disadvantage uplift based on their home postcode.

Each year the LSC publish a disadvantage uplift file for every postcode and SOA, which can be downloaded from their website. Most provider systems will import this file, and automatically assign the correct learner uplift.

Disadvantage uplift for basic skills learners

Learners with programmes made up entirely, or mostly, of basic skills qualifications are entitled to a disadvantage uplift of 12% (1.12). The definition of a basic skills learner for this purpose is relatively complex so the latest LSC funding guidance should be consulted.

Disadvantage uplift for supported accommodation

Learners living in supported accommodation such as foyers, hostels and other forms of managed accommodation providing housing management support are eligible for a disadvantage uplift of 14% (1.14).

Disadvantage uplift for other learners

The following are eligible for a disadvantage uplift of 12% (1.12):

- those living in hostels
- those with mental health problems
- travellers
- those whose statutory education has been interrupted
- those in care or who recently left care
- asylum seekers and refugees eligible for LSC funding
- offenders serving their sentence in the community and ex-offenders
- full-time carers
- those recovering from alcohol or drug dependency
- learners funded by the Single Regeneration Budget.

Note

The disadvantage uplift is potentially tricky to record as providers have to claim it for the right reasons at the right level. There are two fields within the individualised learner record that trigger a claim for disadvantage uplift. Field L32 confirms that a learner is eligible and field L33 identifies the uplift value. If these are not claimed correctly within the learner-responsive model during 2009/10 then the disadvantage uplift in 2011/12 will be incorrect.

Disadvantage uplift for apprenticeships

The disadvantage uplift is also used within the apprenticeship formula.

$$\text{SLN} \times \text{PW} \times \textbf{DU} \times \text{ACU} = \text{apprenticeship funding}$$

This is based on the home postcode of the learner using the same rates as those used for learner-responsive funding. The only difference is that the disadvantage uplift in 2009/10, rather than an average from 2007/08, is used to generate the funding in 2009/10.

Disadvantage uplift for Train to Gain

The disadvantage uplift is not used in the Train to Gain formula.

Area costs uplift

The area costs uplift is one of the elements within the learner-responsive provider factor and is based on the main location of the provider.

$$PW \times DU \times \mathbf{ACU} \times SPM \times SF = provider\ factor$$

The area costs uplift takes account of the 'marked difference in relative cost between London and the South East, and the rest of England'. This makes it a relatively contentious uplift since it can increase funding by as much as 20% and it is not applied anywhere outside of the South East of England. It is also contentious within the South East of England, not least in London where some boroughs gain 12% whilst others gain the maximum 20%. The LSC keeps the uplifts subject to regular review and, apart from the addition of Cambridgeshire, they remain unchanged for 2009/10.

Area costs uplift by location

Location	2009/10 uplift
London A. This includes the boroughs of Camden, Greenwich, Islington, City of London, Kensington and Chelsea, Lambeth, Southwark, Westminster, Wandsworth, Hackney, Tower Hamlets, Lewisham, Newham, Haringey and Hammersmith & Fulham	20%
London B. This includes the boroughs of Barking and Dagenham, Bexley, Havering, Redbridge, Barnet, Enfield, Waltham Forrest, Bromley, Croydon, Kingston upon Thames, Sutton, Brent, Ealing, Harrow, Hillingdon, and Hounslow	12%
Berkshire, Crawley and Surrey	12%
Buckinghamshire and Hertfordshire fringe	10%
Buckinghamshire non-fringe and Oxfordshire	7%
Essex and Kent fringe	6%
Bedfordshire and Hertfordshire non-fringe	3%
Hampshire, Cambridgeshire and Isle of Wight	2%
West Sussex non-fringe	1%
Rest of England	0%

London borough boundaries and the area cost uplift

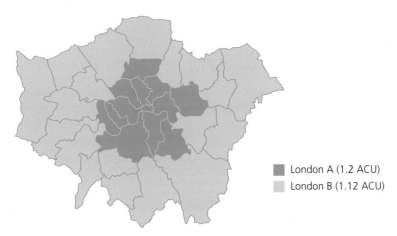

■ London A (1.2 ACU)
■ London B (1.12 ACU)

Exceptional cases

The area costs uplift may change when providers merge, and generally the new uplift is determined by the location of the headquarters of the merged provider. However, in some cases provision is delivered to a wide geographical area, in which case the LSC will calculate a weighted average of the area-costs uplift for each delivery centre.

Employer-responsive

The area costs uplift is also used within the employer-responsive funding formula for both Train to Gain and Apprenticeships.

$$\text{SLN} \times \text{PW} \times \textbf{ACU} = \text{Train to Gain funding}$$

$$\text{SLN} \times \text{PW} \times \text{DU} \times \textbf{ACU} = \text{apprenticeship funding}$$

However, within the employer-responsive funding model the single main location of the provider does not determine the area costs uplift. The area costs uplift is determined by the location of delivery, as recorded within the individualised learner record (ILR). This makes planning the funding for providers that work within the South East of England more difficult as the area costs uplift can change depending on the workplace delivery location.

> **Note**
>
> To aid in the calculation of the employer-responsive area cost uplifts, the LSC publish a file on their website which contains the uplift for every postcode in England. However, the LSC funding software also contains this uplift file, so as long as the delivery postcode is correct then the appropriate area cost uplift will be applied automatically.

Short-programme modifier

The short-programme modifier is one of the elements within the provider factor and for 2009/10 it is based on actual delivery in 2007/08.

$$PW \times DU \times ACU \times \mathbf{SPM} \times SF = \text{provider factor}$$

It was introduced to compensate providers who have a high volume of learners on short programmes of study (defined as less than 225 funded hours in one year). This uplift recognises that there are upfront costs to enrolling learners (marketing, recruitment and so on) and therefore the shorter the course the higher the cost per hour. In a previous funding formula this additional funding was referred to as the entry element.

The short-programme modifier is calculated from the learner level annual SLN, and does not apply to the employer-responsive model nor to Entry to Employment (*see page 88*). In practice the main benefices tend to be adult learner-responsive providers with a high volume of short courses.

Short-programme modifier formula

$$1 + \left(0.3 \times 1 - \left(\frac{\text{Annual SLN}}{0.5} \right) \right)$$

The graph below applies the short-programme modifier formula to the SLN glh to show how in practice a slightly higher SLN value is generated. Beyond 225 SLN glh the short-programme modifier is no longer applied.

Application of the short-programme modifier

The table below shows how this is applied for a single enrolment.

Qualification	SLN glh	Annual SLN
Level 1 BTEC Award in WorkSkills	25	25 / 450 = 0.055

$$1 + \left(0.3 \times 1 - \left(\frac{0.055 \text{ SLN}}{0.5}\right)\right) = 1.2667 \quad \text{Short-programme modifer}$$

In reality many learners enrol on more than one course so the short-programme modifier is applied to the total SLN glh for the learner. The table below reinforces the point that it is at learner level that the short-programme modifier is applied.

Learner programme	SLN glh	SLN
Certificate in Adult Numeracy	45	0.1
Certificate in Adult Literacy	90	0.2
Key skills in ICT	36	0.08
Total programme	**171**	**0.38**

$$1 + \left(0.3 \times 1 - \left(\frac{0.38 \text{ SLN}}{0.5}\right)\right) = 1.0720 \quad \text{Short-programme modifer}$$

Although a short-programme modifier is calculated for every learner, the provider will be assigned a single figure for 2009/10 (such as 1.012) based on the average during delivery in 2007/08. Delivery in 2009/10 will then be the basis for the short-programme modifier assigned for 2011/12. As with all elements of the provider factor, the short-programme modifier is calculated and assigned separately for 16–18 and adult learners.

With the exception of providers who focus on short courses for adults (such as the Working Men's College which had a 10.7% short-programme modifier in 2008/09), the modifier tends to be relatively insignificant once it has been aggregated for use in the provider factor.

Success factor

The success factor is one of the elements within the learner-responsive provider factor and for 2009/10 it is based on actual delivery in 2007/08.

$$PW \times DU \times ACU \times SPM \times \mathbf{SF} = \text{provider factor}$$

The success factor is only used within the learner-responsive funding formula, and has been included so that funding can be reduced for learners who do not complete their course (retention) or pass their qualification (achievement). It takes account of both retention and achievement since it is based on the provider's success rate. The success rate is the retention rate (number completed divided by number started) multiplied by the achievement rate (number passed divided by number completed).

A cap on the maximum amount of funding that can be deducted by the success factor has been set at 50%. This has been achieved by making the success factor the mid-point between the success rate and 100%.

Success factor formula

$$50\% + \frac{\text{Success rate}}{2}$$

This cap and mid-point between the success rate and 100% can also be seen in the graph below.

The relationship between success factor and the success rate

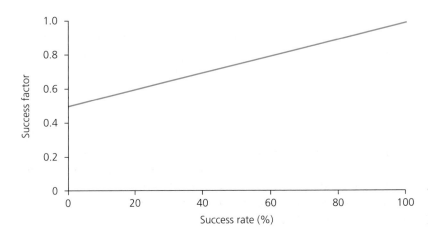

In other words, if a learner fails to both complete and achieve their qualification then only half the total funding is generated. The table below contains an example success factor calculation.

Retention	Achievement	Success rate
80%	90%	80% × 90% = 72%

$$50\% + \frac{72\%}{2} = 0.86 \text{ success factor}$$

The success factor for 2009/10 is fixed before the year begins as it is based on the success rate in 2007/08. However, the relationship between the success rate (a qualitative measure) and the success factor (a funding measure) can helpfully demonstrate the size of impact that learner outcomes have on income. The table below contains a scenario for an individual class in which each learner generates a maximum of £5000.

Learners	Income	Success rate
16 start	£80k planned	16 starts
4 withdraw before completing	£10k lost	12 completed divided by 16 starts = 75% retention
4 that complete do not pass	£10k lost	8 passes divided by 12 completed = 67% achievement
8 achievements in total	£20k lost in total	75% × 67% = 50% success rate (0.75 success factor)

It is also worth noting that the success factor is calculated separately for the 16–18 and adult learner-responsive funding provider factor. Providers may find that their adult success factor is higher than their 16–18 success factor, which can lead to a higher adult provider factor overall. As a result, although the 16–18 national funding rate is higher than the adult rate, the actual weighted funding received per SLN is often greater for the adults.

Additional learning support

Additional learning support is funding for additional activities that provide direct learning support to learners. For example, it may pay for a communication support worker or additional tutor support. ALS is an addition to the final element in the demand-led funding formula.

$$\text{SLN} \times \text{NFR} \times \text{PF} + \textbf{ALS} = \text{Funding}$$

The way that ALS is recorded for 2009/10 in the 16–18 and adult learner-responsive model is unchanged from 2008/09, and detailed information can be found in the LSC's ILR *Funding Compliance Advice 2008/09*.

- The minimum ALS claim for a full-time learner is £501.
- The minimum ALS claim for a part-time learner is £170.
- ALS costs form (below £5500) to be used for low-level claims.
- ALS costs form (above £5500) to be used for high-level claims.
- Claims above £19,000 need to be LSC 'approved in principle'.

However, the way ALS funding is allocated has changed slightly for 2009/10. The first £5500 of high-level claims (claims over £5500 per learner) will no longer be included within the low-level budget. Instead the total amount of the high-level claim will come from the high-level budget, all of which is negotiated between the providers and the LSC based on historical claim data and the number of higher-cost learners planned for the coming year.

Low-level allocations (below £5500 ALS per learner) account for approximately 95% of learners accessing ALS, and 65% of the ALS budget. In 2008/09 one formula for 16–18 and another different formula for adult learner-responsive ALS allocations was introduced to allocate this low-level funding to providers, and it has been used again in 2009/10.

Each formula is designed so that the lower the prior attainment or levels of study, the higher the additional learning support allocation. The concept of this approach is shown in the graph below.

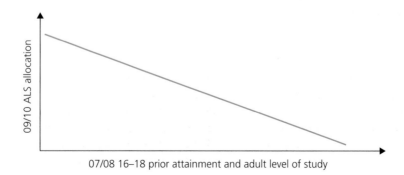

07/08 16–18 prior attainment and adult level of study

The 16–18 ALS allocation formula

To calculate the 16–18 school and college ALS allocations for both colleges and school sixth forms, the LSC have matched 2007/08 provider data with nationally-held GCSE points scores for English and mathematics. A formula is then applied to these scores to ensure that the lower the scores (prior attainment) the higher the ALS allocation.

The adult ALS allocation formula

Prior attainment data is not complete enough to use for adults, so the level of study in 2007/08 is used in a formula to determine the 2009/10 ALS allocation. As the previous diagram illustrated, the lower the average level of study in 2007/08, the higher the ALS allocation will be in 2009/10.

School sixth forms will be allocated their whole ALS budget based on this formula. However, only 60% of the allocation will be made by the formula to colleges with a 16–18 and adult ALS allocation. The remaining 40% will be negotiated with the LSC. This may increase or decrease some ALS allocations significantly between 2008/09 and 2009/10.

2009/10 low-level ALS allocation

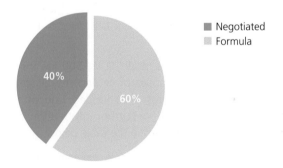

- Negotiated
- Formula

40%
60%

> **Note**
>
> Additional learning support (ALS) should not be confused with learner support funding (LSF). ALS is within the funding models and pays for supporting the learning (such as dyslexia support). LSF is not part of the new funding models and as in previous years, pays for supporting the learner (such as paying for childcare).

The ALS for apprenticeships in 2009/10 within the employer-responsive model does not differ from the arrangements in 2008/09. The ALS for apprenticeships consists of Additional Learning Needs (ALN) funding to support numeracy and literacy and/or Additional Social Needs (ASN) funding to support emotional, behavioural or motivational difficulties. As a result ALS for apprenticeships is also referred to as Additional Learning and Support Needs (ALSN). The LSC does not anticipate that Train to Gain learners will access ALN or ASN, other than in exceptional circumstances.

Allocation examples

These two pages provide examples of how the demand-led formula is applied at allocation level. In order to show how both learner and employer-responsive allocations are set, a fictional further education institution has been created called Pretend College. However, it should be noted that this method of allocating funding is also used for school sixth forms, sixth form colleges and training providers.

In order to calculate the various formula-based allocations for Pretend College it is necessary to set the four values twice within the formula.

1. Standard learner numbers (SLN)   Negotiated with LSC
2. National funding rate (NFR)   Non-negotiable
3. Provider factor (PF)   Non-negotiable
4. Additional learning support (ALS)   40% negotiated with LSC

The learner-responsive funding values for Pretend College are as follows:

Funding model	SLN	NFR	PF	ALS
16–18 learner-responsive	3000	£2920	1.419	£0.8
Adult learner-responsive	2000	£2817	1.523	£1m

Of the 2000 adult learner-responsive model SLNs, 500 are for learners who are expected to pay fees. For the purposes of setting the allocation the reduced funding for these 500 SLNs requires a co-funded rate of £1938 based on £2817 − (£2817 × 47.5% / 1.523). For further information on calculating co-funded rates see page 52. This is shown in the table below.

Funding model	SLN	NFR	PF	ALS
16–18 learner-responsive	3000	£2920	1.419	£0.8m
Adult fully-funded rate	1500	£2817	1.523	£1m
Adult co-funded rate	500	£1938		

Therefore, once the formula SLN × NFR × PF + ALS has been applied, Pretend College has funding allocations for 2009/10 totalling £22m.

Funding model	Provision	ALS	Total
16–18 learner-responsive	£12,430,440	£0.8m	£13,230,440
Adult learner-responsive	£7,911,545	£1m	£8,911,545
Total learner-responsive	**£20,341,985**	**£1.8m**	**£22,141,985**

In addition, following LSC negotiations Pretend College has also been allocated employer-responsive funding for 2009/10.

Employer-responsive funding allocations	Total
16–18 apprenticeships	£2m
19–24 apprenticeships	£1m
25+ apprenticeships	£0.5m
Train to Gain	£3m
Total employer responsive	**£6.5m**

Formula funding of £28.6m for 2008/09 at Pretend College:

16–18 learner-responsive model allocation (excluding apprenticeships) of £13.2m, of which £0.8m is ALS. Actual delivery unlikely to alter the funding received but will be considered for 2010/11 allocation.

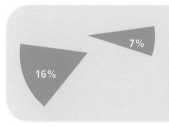

Employer-responsive model
16–18 apprenticeship allocation of £2m, which is paid on delivery.

Adult allocation of £4.5m consists of apprenticeships and Train to Gain funding, which is paid on delivery.

Adult learner-responsive model allocation of £8.9m, of which £1m is additional learning support. The LSC have also set Pretend College tuition fee targets of £669k and, based on performance, may alter the allocation in-year.

Funding cannot be moved between a 16–18 learner-responsive allocation, and an adult learner-responsive or employer-responsive allocation, as they come from two government departments. The Department for Children, Families and Schools (DCSF) funds 16–18 and the new Department for Business, Innovation and Skills (BIS) funds adults (*see page 12*).

The learners

This chapter covers four important funding rules for learners:

Eligibility

Some learners and courses are ineligible for LSC funding, so it is vital before planning a course or enrolling a learner that the eligibility criteria has been met. This section summarises who is and who is not eligible for LSC funding, as well as the types of evidence and records that need to be kept in order to justify the funding claim. It also lists the types of courses which are ineligible for LSC funding. However, eligibility is a complex area and it is always advisable to refer to the detailed eligibility guidance published by the LSC. The LSC also has some discretion in this area, so if in doubt or seeking a solution it is always best to contact them.

Fee element

Many adult learners are ineligible for fee remission funding, which means the funding is reduced by a fee element. This section summarises how the fee element has risen in recent years to be more than double that in 2004/05, which may explain why some provider's tuition fees have risen so fast. The formula for the fee element deduction within the learner (unweighted) and employer (weighted) funding models is then explained. Finally, the co-funded rate, which is simply the funding rate for adults that do not receive fee remission funding, and the co-funding formula are explained.

Minimum attendance

Learners need to pass a minimum attendance period before they can be defined as a start, generate funding, and count towards targets. There are three minimum attendance periods used in all three funding models. This section describes these periods, along with the definitions of start dates, planned end dates, and perhaps most importantly in this context, the withdrawal date (last date of attendance). This counting methodology is quite different from methods used before 2008/09, which included fixed census dates. In terms of full-time learners the significance of this is looked at in detail, as withdrawals in October may no longer generate funding nor count towards targets.

SLN per learner ratio

The LSC is keen on ratios, as it uses them to make comparisons between providers, to consider value for money, and as a basis for negotiating future funding allocations. This section looks at the SLN per learner ratio (or simply SLN ratio). Since SLNs are an unweighted unit of cost for the LSC, they are keen to avoid the average cost of learners (SLN per learner) rising. The aim is to keep public spending under control and stop providers expanding learners' programme size, which would increase the SLN per learner ratio. However, this section considers evidence which suggests the SLN per learner ratio will inevitably rise as a consequence of providers altering their mix and balance of provision to deliver government targets and LSC priority provision.

Eligibility

Not all courses, nor learners, are eligible for LSC funding. Therefore, before planning a course or enrolling a learner, it important that providers establish whether they are eligible. The LSC funding guidance, available at www.lsc.gov.uk, contains the detailed eligibility rules.

It can be difficult to determine whether a learner or course is eligible for LSC funding, so it is always recommended that providers:
* identify a member of staff as the eligibility expert, who keeps up to date with the rules, evidence and audit requirements;
* consult the LSC on a case-by-case basis when in doubt;
* consult the LSC if they believe that an ineligible learner or course should be considered for funding in exceptional circumstances.

Learner eligibility
The following summarises just some of the learner eligibility rules, but providers should always consult the detailed LSC guidance.

Eligible for LSC Funding	Ineligible for LSC Funding
'Home' learners with 'ordinary residence' for 3 years preceding academic year (defined by LSC)	'Overseas' learners, who are defined as not meeting the 'home' learner criteria
Asylum seekers legally in the UK	Person subject to deportation order
Those above 'compulsory school age' and resident in England	Those of 'compulsory school age' or resident outside England
Those enrolled on a Level 4 or 5 course not funded by HEFCE	Those currently enrolled on a higher-education course funded by HEFCE
Provider employees studying outside working hours, plus basic skills provision in working hours	Provider employees studying in working hours (except basic teaching qualifications for teachers or trainers, who are eligible)
Full-time learners enrolled with one provider at any given time	Those funded by the LSC as full-time learners at another provider
All learners detained in prison	

Course eligibility

In order to claim LSC funding, providers are required to maintain records of learner existence and eligibility. The LSC outlines the detailed requirements within its funding guidance, which as a minimum include signed records of:
- learning agreements;
- enrolment forms;
- learner records of attendance;
- achievement evidence.

In order to claim funding for courses, providers must send enrolment information to the LSC, as data within an individualised learner record (ILR). Each enrolment requires an eight-digit code known as the 'learning aim', which identifies the course the learner is enrolled on. Only those learning aims that are eligible for LSC funding can be submitted within an ILR claim. Therefore, when planning a course it is advisable to first check eligibility on the Learning Aim Database (LAD).

When planning a course, the LAD can also be used to determine:
- the listed SLN or SLN glh funding rates;
- the programme weighting for the learner or employer model;
- whether the qualification contributes to government targets;
- whether the qualification is eligible for automatic fee remission.

See page 138 for more information about the LAD.

Learner, course and enrolment data: path to eligible funding

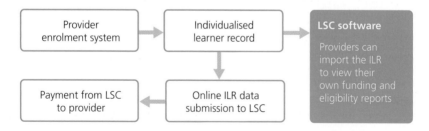

Provision ineligible for LSC funding generally includes:
- vendor-certificated qualifications (e.g. Microsoft);
- courses of fewer than nine guided learning hours, except for adults when the qualification is on the National Qualifications Framework (NQF);
- additional or optional units beyond the minimum required;
- single units for adults outside the QCF trials (*see page 104 and 132*);
- company-specific knowledge courses;
- courses for 16–18-year-olds not approved under section 96;
- qualification resits and stand-alone courses designed to meet employers' statutory or other responsibilities.

The fee element and the co-funded rate

Many adult learners, particularly those who are employed, are ineligible for full funding because it is assumed they will pay tuition fees. In 2009/10 the LSC will deduct 47.5% of the unweighted (learner model) or weighted (employer model) funding. The fee element percentage has been rising year on year and is now 124% more than in 2004/05.

Rising fee element (funding deducted for fee payers)

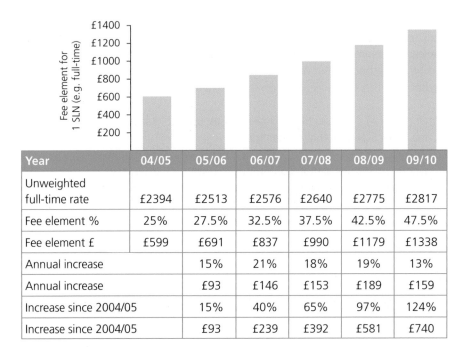

Year	04/05	05/06	06/07	07/08	08/09	09/10
Unweighted full-time rate	£2394	£2513	£2576	£2640	£2775	£2817
Fee element %	25%	27.5%	32.5%	37.5%	42.5%	47.5%
Fee element £	£599	£691	£837	£990	£1179	£1338
Annual increase		15%	21%	18%	19%	13%
Annual increase		£93	£146	£153	£189	£159
Increase since 2004/05		15%	40%	65%	97%	124%
Increase since 2004/05		£93	£239	£392	£581	£740

As shown in the table above, the fee element has more than doubled within five years, which means not only has the funding reduction more than doubled, but tuition fees would also have to more than double to maintain overall income levels. The LSC can and do set total tuition fee income targets based on the fee deduction, but they cannot dictate the individual tuition fees that providers set as this would fall foul of competition law.

Note

Providers should not set fee levels that approach the value of the LSC funding that would be generated by multiplying the SLN value, programme weighting, area cost uplift and national funding rate. In these cases providers should not claim LSC funding, nor should they need to.

Adult learner-responsive funding model fee element

The table below contains an example fee element using the national funding rate of £2817. In the adult learner-responsive funding model, the calculation is unweighted (excludes the provider factor), so the fee element would be the same for all providers regardless of, for example, location.

Example enrolment	Fee element
Full-time NVQ with listed SLN glh of 520	520 / 450 × £2817 × 47.5% = £1546

Using this formula it is possible to say that in 2009/10 the tuition fee for all learners is £2.97 per funded hour, as shown in the equation below.

$$(1 / 450) \times £2817 \times 47.5\% = £2.97 \text{ per hour}$$

However, it should be remembered that the fee element is based on the SLN glh, which if listed may not be the same as the duration that the provider actually delivers (see page 28).

Adult learner-responsive co-funded rate

The co-funded rate is important as it is the rate used for fee-paying learners within the adult learner-responsive allocation (see page 46). It is used in the formula and replaces the national funding rate as follows:

SLN × **co-funded rate** × provider factor = funding for fee payers

The co-funded rate formula is:

co-funded rate = NFR − (NFR × 47.5% / provider factor)

Employer-responsive funding model fee element

The fee element (or employer contribution) to be deducted from Train to Gain and apprenticeship funding is always a percentage of the full (weighted) funding.

When applicable, the Train to Gain fee element is 47.5% in 2009/10.

Train to Gain	Fee element (employer funding model)
NVQ Level 3	0.644 × £2901 × PW × ACU × 47.5% = fee element

The deduction for all 19+ (adult) apprenticeship frameworks is also in the region of 47.5%. However, the exact percentage applied to each enrolment within an apprenticeship framework varies (see page 122). The fee percentage, such as 17.5% for key skill qualifications, can be found within the Learning Aim Database (see page 138).

Minimum attendance

Minimum attendance is also referred to as 'the definition of a start' or 'when they count'. In funding terms, it is the minimum duration of on-programme learning activities required for funding to be claimed. If the learner withdraws from the enrolment before this minimum period then funding cannot be claimed, nor can the learner be counted towards LSC targets.

The minimum attendance rules are the same across all three funding models, as described within the table below.

Course duration	Minimum attendance
24 weeks or more	6 weeks
2 – 24 weeks	2 weeks
Less than 2 weeks	1 attendance

The course duration is based on the number of calendar days between the start date and planned end date of the enrolment. The attendance duration is then measured by the distance between the start date and the actual end date. If the attendance duration is less than the minimum attendance, funding will not be generated.

Note

The withdrawal date is the last date of attendance as recorded on the enrolment register. It is not the date in which the learner informs the provider they will no longer be participating, nor a given period such as four weeks after the final attendance, nor the date when the data is changed.

The diagram below highlights the three minimum attendance periods for a one-week, 18-week, and full-year course. In these examples, all the courses start in the first term, when the first learning activity typically takes place in the middle of September.

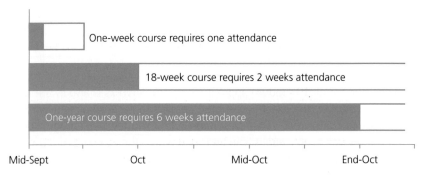

Within the 16–18 and adult learner-responsive funding models, once the minimum attendance period has been achieved the provider can claim the full SLN. Within the employer-responsive funding model, the minimum attendance rules are the same, but monthly instalments only continue while the learner is on-programme and 25% is held back for achievement.

If an enrolment period spans two academic years, then a second minimum attendance period must be passed (starting from 1 August in the second year). Failure to pass this second period means the annualised funding (based on calendar days per year) cannot be claimed for the second year.

For example, a full-time two-year course such as the BTEC National Diploma might begin on 1 August 2009 and end on 31 July 2011. The learner would need to attend until at least six weeks into the second year (middle of September 2010) for full funding to be claimed.

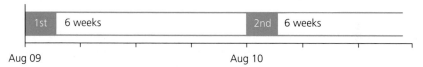

The example above is relatively simple because by starting in August and finishing in July the funding is exactly 50% for each year (excluding inflation). In reality, courses of this nature usually start in the middle of September, so the funding split is unlikely to be exactly 50% for each year.

Note

Many courses in the second year begin in mid-September. This means if a learner withdraws during the summer but the withdrawal date is incorrectly recorded at the start of the second year, all of the funding will be claimed. Providers need to be particularly careful to avoid this.

This definition of a start is significantly different from that used for 2008/09. Previously, full-time learners starting in September had to be in learning after 1 October to count. The change to a six-week minimum attendance now means that traditional full-time learners starting in the middle of September have a far longer minimum attendance period.

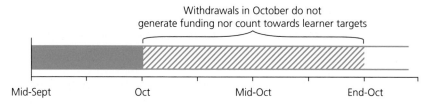

Caution is therefore advised when setting targets or making learner number comparisons which include the pre-2008/09 counting methodology.

SLN per learner ratio

Ratios are important as they are used by the LSC to make judgements about the relative costs of provision and to inform allocations and targets. In the past, funding per full-time equivalent (FTE) was a popular ratio with the LSC, but it was not without its critics who highlighted that:

- FTEs are not well understood nor does the funding per FTE ratio take account of learner participation;
- FTEs are based on actual glh, which was a problem for the workplace NVQs as they have relatively few glh;
- funding per FTE includes weightings, so a rising ratio might simply be a result of increased success rates.

The introduction of standard learner numbers (SLN) in 2008/09 presented the opportunity to introduce a new ratio. The SLN per learner ratio has become an important measure, as it describes the average unweighted value of each learner. Put simply, the higher the ratio, the fewer learners can share the same pot of funding. This is important, and the LSC have stated in their *Statement of Priorities for 2008/09 to 2010/11* that 'to offer opportunities for as many learners as possible we need to control unit cost increases, including those arising from the expansion of learners' programmes'.

A provider delivering larger programmes to the same number of learners is perhaps the most obvious reason for an increase in the SLN per learner ratio. In the example below, the ratio has increased by 7% from 1.08 to 1.16 simply by delivering an additional key skills qualification.

Programme	SLN	Programme	SLN
BTEC First Diploma	1	BTEC First Diploma	1
1 key skill	0.08	2 key skills	0.16
SLN per learner ratio	1.08	SLN per learner ratio	1.16

This approach is naturally unpopular with the LSC, particularly as their funds are limited and they want to avoid rising unit costs. The LSC response is generally to cap the SLN per learner ratio when negotiating funding allocations. However, the average value of both 16–18 and adult learners has been rising for a number of years, and is likely to continue to do so for the foreseeable future.

The available evidence suggests that a rising SLN per learner ratio has less to do with providers expanding learners' programmes, and more to do with the Government's prioritisation of funding for both higher-value full-time 16–18-year-olds and target-bearing adults.

16–18 full-time growth with part-time reductions

In recent years, the LSC has shown less interest in full- and part-time participation trends, and only set total participation targets for providers. Although total participation may not change, often full-time learners are increasing as part-time learners are decreasing. As a result, the average learner value (SLN per learner ratio) will inevitably increase. This is demonstrated in the table below, with actual LSC projected learners and some example SLN per learner ratios which remain constant for full-timers (1.5) and part-timers (0.5), yet increase year on year when combined.

LSC projected learners		2008/09	2009/10	2010/11
16–18 full-time	learners ('000)	660	664	666
16–18 part-time	learners ('000)	113	109	107
Total	**learners ('000)**	**773**	**773**	**773**

Example SLNs		2008/09	2009/10	2010/11
16–18 full-time	SLN per learner	1.5	1.5	1.5
16–18 part-time	SLN per learner	0.5	0.5	0.5
Total ratio	**SLN per learner**	**1.354**	**1.359**	**1.362**

Adults on higher-value and priority qualifications

Although overall investment in adult provision has remained relatively stable, a stark consequence of the Government's prioritisation of adult funding towards skills has been a significant overall reduction in adult learners. The reason for this was candidly described and predicted by the Government in October 2005:

> We are broadly maintaining the overall public funding that the LSC will be able to allocate to support adult learning but the pattern of that learning will change. To meet our national priorities, we need to shift the pattern so that we provide longer and more expensive courses for adults. So while maintaining the overall volume of adult funding, we estimate there will be a net reduction in publicly-funded places of around 230,000 (about 6%).
>
> Source: *LSC Grant Letter 2006/07*, DfES (October 2005)

For example, a provider could fund 1000 learners on low priority short courses with an SLN per learner ratio of 0.1 or 200 learners on a first full Level 2 with an SLN per learner ratio of 0.5. Therefore, as providers alter their mix and balance to deliver government targets, the average value of the learner (SLN per learner ratio) will increase, often substantially.

School funding

School sixth form funding comes from the LSC, and for individual qualifications the amount is calculated using the LSC's demand-led funding formula (*see page 27*). However, the LSC provides funding to local authorities to forward to schools with sixth forms – it does not directly fund schools. Local authorities can reduce or add to the funding within both the LSC allocation and the school's non-age-weighted pupil funding.

The 2009/10 funding allocation process for schools

Source: *School Sixth Form Guidance*, LSC (June 2009)

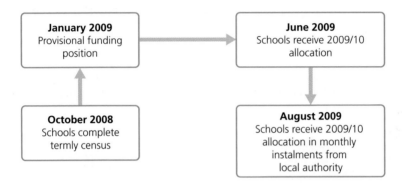

The graph and list below shows that in 2008/09 the average school sixth form had an allocation of £1m for just over 200 learners.

2008/09 school sixth form learner allocations

Source: *LSC Allocations Spreadsheet*

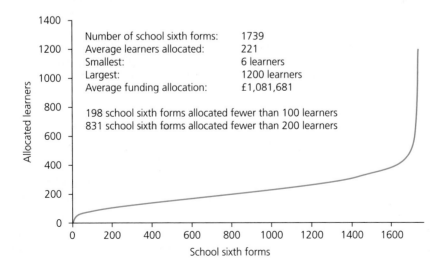

Number of school sixth forms: 1739
Average learners allocated: 221
Smallest: 6 learners
Largest: 1200 learners
Average funding allocation: £1,081,681

198 school sixth forms allocated fewer than 100 learners
831 school sixth forms allocated fewer than 200 learners

Key features

School sixth forms are funded using the demand-led learner-responsive funding formula (*see page 27*). The qualifications which are eligible for 16–18 learner-responsive funding are determined by the LSC, and can be found within the Learning Aim Database (*see page 138*). In some cases learning aims are eligible for 16–18 funding but not for 19+ funding (and vice versa). In the case of school sixth forms, all qualifications have a listed rate (*see page 29*).

A shortened version of the LSC funding guidance has been produced for school sixth forms for 2009/10. Additional details, such as learner eligibility, can be found in the 2008/09 booklets (*see page 15*).

Funding formula

School sixth forms use the same formula used for 16–18-year-olds and adult learners. However, the national funding rate (NFR) is different for school sixth form provision (*see page 30*).

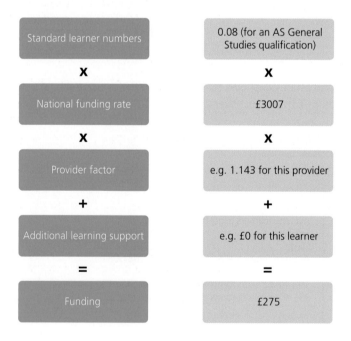

This chapter includes examples of unweighted funding for a range of courses. Unweighted means the SLN value has only been multiplied by the national funding rate. Thus, for a school sixth form in 2009/10 the unweighted funding would be SLN multiplied by £3007. The same principle, with a different national funding rate, applies for 16–18 provision in colleges (£2920) and adult learner-responsive provision (£2817).

Key changes for 2009/10

The LSC have published funding guidance specifically for school sixth forms, which highlights the key changes for 2009/10.

Change type	Change description
Transitional protection	The policy for 2009/10 was that no school would have a national rate of more than £3007 + 2.1% per SLN. However, when transitional protection was calculated a number of schools had a rate higher than £4000 per SLN. The LSC have therefore put in place steps to accelerate convergance to the national rate. Schools with a transitional rate in 2009/10 (a rate higher than £3007) should consult the LSC funding guidance for full details.
Success rates	The school sixth form calculation of the success rate factor used in the 2009/10 allocation was based on a retention rate for Year 12 and a success rate for Year 13 and Year 14 learners. Success rate is retention rate multiplied by achievement rate.
Final 2009/10 allocations	The DCSF have asked the LSC to be kept informed of any individual school recruitment issues from September. This could mean that allocations are revised in-year.
Definition of full-time and eligibility for entitlement funding	Full-time is to be defined as being on a course of 450 glh (1 SLN) or more in a year. This includes the entitlement of 114 glh (0.25 SLN), therefore other qualifications in the learner's programme must total at least 336 glh (0.75 SLN) to qualify for entitlement (*see page 68*).
Recording data	With the new approach to success-rate calculations it is important that the start and end dates (both expected and actual end dates) and the completion status for each qualification are completed accurately.
Foundation Learning	Any school sixth form wishing to deliver foundation learning should follow the principles (*see page 74*). Only those qualifications accredited on the QCF and authorised for funding by the LSC are fundable and they must all be individually recorded on the school census.

GCSE curriculum

General Certificates of Secondary Education (GCSEs) were first introduced in 1986 to replace O-levels and Certificates of Secondary Education (CSEs). In 1996 the Short Course GCSE was introduced (half the size and funding) and in 2002 the Applied GCSE was introduced (double the size and funding). In 2005/06 school sixth forms and colleges claimed approximately £0.6m for Short Course GCSEs, £110m for GCSEs and £6m for Applied GCSEs.

Although GCSEs are generally studied at school in Years 10 and 11 (14- and 15-year-olds) they are also popular within post-16 education, particularly as part of a progression pathway to Level 3 and university.

The funding for GCSEs is calculated using the learner-responsive funding formula, as outlined on page 27. The listed SLN glh is divided by 450 to determine the SLN, which is then multiplied by the school sixth form national funding rate of £3007 to determine the unweighted funding.

GCSE listed rates and funding when studied during the day

GCSE SLNs (day)	SLN glh	SLN	Unweighted funding
Short Course GCSE	50	0.111	£334
GCSE	100	0.222	£668
Applied GCSE	200	0.444	£1336

Some learners also study GCSEs during the evening, which usually requires fewer teaching hours. Therefore, the LSC has two listed funding rates for each GCSE with an evening rate 40% lower than the day rate.

GCSE listed rates and funding when studied during the evening

GCSE SLNs (evening)	SLN glh	SLN	Unweighted funding
Short Course GCSE	30	0.067	£200
GCSE	60	0.133	£401
Applied GCSE	120	0.267	£802

Sixth form colleges and general further education colleges would receive 3% less unweighted funding for 16–18-year-olds, since the national funding rate in 2009/10 is £2920. Adults would receive 6% less funding with a national funding rate of £2817 (see page 30). Also, the funding would be deducted by a further 47.5% for adults who were fee-paying (see page 52).

GCSEs are usually taught over two years, in which case the funding is claimed in both years in proportion to the number of days the learner is on-programme in each academic year (see page 54).

The table below is an example of how funding in 2009/10 might be claimed for a Year 10 (first year) GCSE programme at a school sixth form.

Example 2-year programme	SLN glh	SLN	09/10 SLN	Unweighted funding
11 GCSEs	1100	2.444	1.222	£3675

GCSEs may also form part of a programme of study which contains other qualifications, such as the BTEC First Certificate (see page 84). The table below shows an unweighted funding example for a one-year programme.

Example programme	SLN glh	SLN	Unweighted funding
4 GCSEs	400	0.889	£2673
1 BTEC First Diploma	225	0.5	£1504
Total	625	1.389	£4177

Supplementary information about GCSEs:
• GCSEs have a two-tier structure in terms of levels of attainment, with grades D-G equivalent to Level 1 (foundation) and grades A*-C equivalent to Level 2 (higher).

• GCSEs have the 'potential to contribute' to the Government's full Level 2 Public Service Agreement (PSA) target (see page 13). This is because the NQF definition of a full Level 2 is 'equivalent to 5 GCSEs at grades A*-C'. Therefore, every GCSE is allocated 20% of a full Level 2 within the Learning Aim Database and consequently categorised by the LSC as a priority qualification.

• GCSEs in English and mathematics contribute to the Government's Skills for Life PSA target. Yet, unlike most other numeracy and literacy qualifications, they are neither eligible for fee remission nor the basic skills programme weighting and disadvantage uplift.

• GCSEs in English and mathematics grade A*-C are 'proxy qualifications' for key skills in communication and application of number. This means the learner is exempt from the relevant key skill test. GCSE Computing, GCSE Information Systems and GCSE ICT qualifications are proxy qualifications for key skills in ICT.

A-level curriculum

The General Certificate in Education (GCE) at Advanced Level (A-level) was introduced in 1951. In 2000 the Government introduced Curriculum 2000 which split the six-unit A-level into a three-unit AS (Advanced Subsidiary) and three-unit A2. In 2005 A-levels in applied subjects were introduced to replace the Advanced Vocational Certificate of Education (AVCE), and in 2008 a new A* grade was introduced for A2 level exam results above 90%. A-levels are traditionally studied by 16–18-year-olds in school sixth forms, sixth form colleges and further education colleges after completing GCSEs. They are also studied in the evening by about 50,000 adults, which usually requires fewer teaching hours.

A-level funding rates are complicated by three factors:

1. The listed rate for AS and A2 General Studies, which on average is only taught in one hour per week, is 76% less than for other AS and A2 qualifications. The LSC also considered reducing the rate for AS and A2 Critical Thinking and will consider it again for 2010/11.

2. As with GCSEs, the AS and A2 evening rate is 60% lower than the day rate (with the exception of AS and A2 General Studies).

3. Unlike GCSEs, the Applied AS and A2 qualifications are not simply double the A-level rate.

The funding for A-levels is calculated using the learner-responsive funding formula, as outlined on page 27. All the A-level qualifications have a listed SLN glh on the LAD (*see page 138*) which is divided by 450 to calculate the SLN. The SLN is then multiplied by the national funding rate (£3007 for school sixth forms) to determine the unweighted funding.

A-level listed rates and funding when studied during the day

A-level SLNs (day)	SLN glh	SLN	Unweighted funding
AS or A2 excl. General Studies	150	0.333	£1002
AS or A2 General Studies	36	0.08	£241
Applied AS or A2	180	0.4	£1203
Applied A-level	360	0.8	£2406
Applied AS or A2 Double Award	450	1	£3007
Applied A-level Double Award	900	2	£6014

A-level listed rates and funding when studied during the evening

A-level SLNs (evening)	SLN glh	SLN	Unweighted funding
AS or A2 excl. General Studies	90	0.2	£601
AS or A2 General Studies	36	0.08	£241
Applied AS or A2	108	0.24	£722
Applied A-level	216	0.48	£1443
Applied AS or A2 Double Award	270	0.6	£1804
Applied A-level Double Award	540	1.2	£3608

The table below is an example of how funding might be claimed for a first year A-level programme at a school sixth form.

A-level programme of study	SLN glh	SLN	Unweighted funding
AS History	150	0.333	£1001
AS Politics	150	0.333	£1001
AS Economics	150	0.333	£1001
AS General Studies	36	0.08	£241
Key skills in communication	36	0.08	£241
Entitlement (see page 68)	114	0.253	£762
Total	636	1.412	£4247

This final table shows each type of A-level qualification, and their contribution towards the full Level 3 PSA target (see page 13).

A-level	Percentage contribution to a full Level 3
AS or A2 (incl. General Studies)	25%
Applied AS or A2	25%
Applied A-level	50%
Applied AS or A2 Double Award	50%
Applied A-level Double Award	100%

The International Baccalaureate

The International Baccalaureate (IB) Diploma is a two-year qualification at Level 3 designed to lead to progression to university, and is studied predominantly by 16–19-year-old learners. In 2006/07 the IB Diploma was delivered by 17 colleges and 25 school sixth forms across 32 local authorities, and demand for the IB continues to rise.

The IB Diploma qualification consists of six certificates and learners usually study three at higher level (240 glh) and three at standard level (150 glh):
1. Own language
2. Second language
3. Individuals and society (e.g. history)
4. The arts
5. Experimental sciences
6. Mathematics and computer science.

There are also three compulsory core requirements:
1. Extended essay (4,000 words)
2. Theory of knowledge
3. Creativity, action, service.

The certificates are scored out of seven and each core element is worth one point (with up to a further additional three points depending on grades). A minimum of 24 points are required to be awarded the IB Diploma and the highest total that a Diploma learner can be awarded is 45 points. The IB Diploma UCAS tariff points were recently revised down. They range from 260 for 24 points to 720 for 45 points.

The full IB Diploma is credited as offering a broader mix of subjects than most A-level programmes. As such it is funded as a large single programme, and the table below shows how the elements might be delivered alongside standard 16–18 tutorial and enrichment activities.

Example IB Programme	Guided learning hours over two years
3 higher level certificates	720
3 standard level certificates	450
Extended essay	n/a
Theory of knowledge	128
Creativity, action, service	128
Tutorials and other enrichment activities	152
Total guided learning hours	1578

When setting the funding rates for the IB Diploma, the LSC took account of the 114 SLN glh per year entitlement for the 16–18-year-old tutorial and enrichment activities (*see page 68*). Therefore, they have deducted 228glh from the 1578glh and listed the IB Diploma qualification rate at 1350glh.

IB Diploma listed rate	1350 SLN glh / 450 = 3 SLN

The unweighted and uncapped funding for the IB Diploma would be:

3 SLN × £3007 school sixth form funding rate = £9021

With entitlement (*see page 68*) the funding increases as follows:

IB Diploma Programme	SLN glh	SLN	Unweighted funding
International Baccalaureate	1350	3	£9021
Entitlement (2 years)	228	0.507	£1524
Total SLN and funding	**3.507**	**3.507**	**£10,545***

However, the IB Diploma is a two-year programme. This means funding in 2009/10 is based on the proportion of days the learner is on-programme (*see page 54*). The first year of the programme would therefore generate approximately half the total funding.

IB Diploma Programme (year 1)	SLN glh	SLN	Unweighted funding
International Baccalaureate	675	1.5	£4511
Entitlement (2 years)	114	0.253	£762
Total SLN and funding	**789**	**1.753**	**£5272***

* The LSC have attempted to list the SLNs that would generate maximum funding. However, the 3.507 total SLN very slightly exceeds the learner SLN cap of 3.5 (1.75 per year). Therefore, the unweighted funding for a school sixth form would actually be £10,525 over two years (excluding inflation). Also, SLN values are allocated to each academic year based on the percentage of calendar days (between enrolment start and end date) in the given year. Therefore, to avoid one of the years further exceeding the 1.75 SLN cap, the number of calendar days in the first year would need to be identical to the number of days in the second year.

Entitlement

Funding for 16–18 entitlement was introduced in 2000/01 to support a new approach to 16–18 education (Curriculum 2000). This included funding to ensure that all 16–18-year-old learners acquired skills in literacy, numeracy and IT as well as for regular tutorials and enrichment activities which are in addition to the qualifications within a learners programme. In 2008/09 the element of funding for the tutorials and enrichment activities was funded separately as 'entitlement'.

Learners eligible for entitlement

Entitlement funding may be claimed for learners who are both:

- aged under 19 on 31 August in the teaching year in which they start their programme of study;

- studying on a full-time basis, as defined by the LSC ('enrolled on a programme of at least 450 glh in any 12-month period'). This includes the entitlement hours, which are assumed by the LSC to be 114 glh per year. However, the expectation is that 'full-time programmes for 16–18-year-olds will be substantially greater than the minimum threshold level'.

Expectations when entitlement is claimed

When claiming entitlement funding the LSC also state that 'in line with ministers' expectations, learners are expected to be':

- on programmes which are substantially greater than the minimum threshold for full-time;

- aiming to achieve any of the relevant QCA (now QCDA) key (or functional) skill qualifications at Level 2 (Communication, Application of Number and/or IT) that they have not already achieved at GCSE grades A*–C or equivalent. This implies that learners are expected to register with the awarding body, take the end test and submit their portfolio for each key skill taken. Learners studying GCSEs in appropriate subjects are exempt from this requirement;

- aiming to achieve one relevant Level 3 key skills qualification if the intention is for the learner to pursue a professional or higher qualification;

- undertaking some key skills learning as part of the overall entitlement package where government expectations outlined above have already been met;

- for a small minority of learners, basic skills certificates may be more appropriate than key skills. However, disadvantage uplift for basic skills learners should not apply in these situations (*see page 36*).

Enrichment activities

In addition to tutorials, it is expected that entitlement funding will be used to fund enrichment activities. These might include:

- delivery not otherwise funded (such as Duke of Edinburgh awards);

- careers guidance;

- sports, music, dance and drama;

- industry-related programmes, including vendor-certificated qualifications that would not otherwise be funded;

- health education;

- use of learning resource centres;

- in exceptional cases part-time jobs or work-experience may be considered as enrichment activity within entitlement funding.

Entitlement funding

The entitlement funding is claimed for the learner, at a listed rate of 114 SLN glh per year. Together with a key skills qualification funded at 36 SLN glh, it is equivalent to the teaching time expected for an AS-level over one year.

Example programme with entitlement funding	SLN glh	SLN	Unweighted funding
AS-level Chemistry	150	0.333	£1002
AS-level Biology	150	0.333	£1002
AS-level Physics	150	0.333	£1002
AS-level Mathematics	150	0.333	£1002
Key skills in ICT	36	0.08	£241
Entitlement	114	0.253	£762
Total	750	1.667	£5012

> **Note**
>
> Entitlement funding is included with the annual SLN cap of 1.75 (*see page 28*). Hence, the total annual SLN value of the qualifications must be less than 1.5 (1.75 − 0.253) if all the entitlement funding is to be claimed.

16–18 college funding

This chapter includes a number of qualifications and programmes which are fundable for 16–18-year-olds in the learner-responsive funding model (*see page 16*).

The range of providers

The great majority of 16–18 learner-responsive funding (excluding school sixth forms) is allocated to further education (FE) colleges, hence the name of this chapter. However, there are a number of other providers with 16–18 learner-responsive allocations, such as local authorities and private training providers delivering Entry to Employment (*see page 88*). Every provider with a 16–18 learner-responsive allocation, regardless of type, is funded using the demand-led funding formula (*see page 27*).

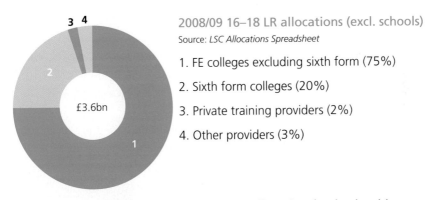

2008/09 16–18 LR allocations (excl. schools)
Source: *LSC Allocations Spreadsheet*

1. FE colleges excluding sixth form (75%)

2. Sixth form colleges (20%)

3. Private training providers (2%)

4. Other providers (3%)

£3.6bn

2008/09 16–18 learner-responsive average allocation (excl. schools)
Source: *LSC Allocations Spreadsheet*

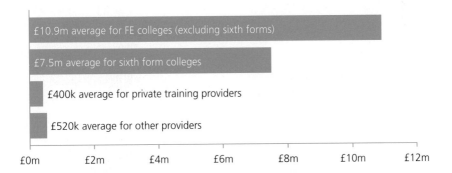

£10.9m average for FE colleges (excluding sixth forms)

£7.5m average for sixth form colleges

£400k average for private training providers

£520k average for other providers

£0m   £2m   £4m   £6m   £8m   £10m   £12m

The range of provision

This chapter includes examples of qualifications and programmes which can be funded from 16–18 learner-responsive allocations. Other qualifications within the school and adult college funding chapters can also be funded. However, it is important to apply the 16–18 college funding formula elements, such as the national funding rate of £2920 in 2009/10.

Key features

To be eligible for 16–18 learner-responsive funding in 2009/10 the learner must be 18 or younger on 31 August 2009 and satisfy the LSC learner eligibility requirements (*see page 50*). Learners who are 19 on 31 August with a start date in 2008/09 (when they were 18) are funded at 16–18 rates but contribute to adult learner-responsive (ALR) targets and generate funding from the ALR allocation (*see page 94*).

The qualifications and courses which are eligible for 16–18 learner-responsive funding are determined by the LSC, and can be found within the Learning Aim Database (*see page 138*). In some cases learning aims are eligible for 16–18 funding but not for 19+ funding (and vice versa).

Funding formula

16–18 colleges use the same formula used for school sixth forms and adult learner-responsive learners. The national funding rate (NFR), however, is different to 16–18 college provision (*see page 30*).

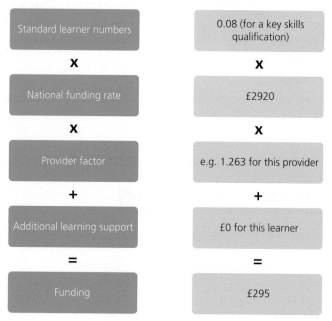

Standard learner numbers	0.08 (for a key skills qualification)
X	X
National funding rate	£2920
X	X
Provider factor	e.g. 1.263 for this provider
+	+
Additional learning support	£0 for this learner
=	=
Funding	£295

The provision within this chapter includes examples of unweighted funding. This means the SLN value has only been multiplied by the national funding rate. Thus, for 16–18 college funding in 2009/10 the unweighted funding would be SLN multiplied by £2920. The same principle, with a different national funding rate, applies for 16–18 provision in schools (£3007) and adult learner-responsive provision in colleges (£2817).

National rates

As outlined on page 28, where a qualification rate (SLN glh) is listed it is divided by 450 to determine the SLN value. A-levels and GCSEs have a day and evening rate (*see pages 62 and 64*). When the Learning Aim Database does not have a listed rate, the size of the provider's programme (glh) is divided by 450 to calculate the SLN value. Also:

- each learner programme has an annualised SLN cap of 1.75 (equivalent to 787.5 SLN glh);
- funding for an enrolment will only be generated if the minimum attendance period has been passed (*see page 54*);
- the following pages include examples of unweighted funding, which in 2009/10 is calculated as SLN × £2920. Unweighted funding for school sixth forms would be SLN × £3007.

Rates for consortia

The new 14–19 Diploma (*see page 76*) is designed to be delivered by a range of providers within a consortium. For this reason, the rates include an uplift of approximately 5% to contribute to the cost of collaboration and work experience. The LSC recommend that this funding is pooled to cover the additional cost of collaboration such as joint timetabling, work experience, employer engagement and health and safety. In addition, since all the funding flows to the home provider, consortia may need to agree local approaches to the distribution of the funding.

The baseline calculation for purchasing components of the Diploma should start with the LSC-published SLN values and programme weightings. Consortia will then need to agree local rates for delivery to reflect local circumstances.

Schools and colleges will have bespoke rates because of their different provider factors and different national funding rates. Therefore using a purely formulaic approach may not always lead to a fair allocation between consortia members, i.e. where the programme weighting for the off-site delivery is higher than that recognised in the school's provider factor. Consortia will therefore need to agree their local approach and allow for the circumstances listed below:

- which provider's premises are to be used

- proportion of learning that is workshop, laboratory or classroom-based

- whether quid pro quo arrangements would save additional costs and bureaucracy

- the programme weighting of the learning aim being purchased

- the impact of the success rates on funding, and if any funding should be withheld until the qualification is achieved.

Source: *Funding Guidance 2009/10*, Update v4.0, LSC (July 2009)

Foundation Learning

Foundation Learning (FL) (previously Foundation Learning Tier (FLT)) is used to describe a range of provision and learning at Entry Level and Level 1 for both 14–19-year-olds and adults. Introduced as a pilot in 2008/09, FL has moved into implementation phase for 2009/10 and is expected to be fully operational in 2010/11.

> Foundation Learning is all about progression, with learners and practitioners jointly agreeing an intended 'destination', wherever possible to Level 2 (Diploma, Apprenticeships, GCSEs) or for some learners, independent living or supported employment. With the right level of support all but a very small minority of learners will have the capacity to progress to positive outcomes. Qualifications that support Foundation Learning offer more flexible opportunities for learners to achieve and progress; this includes 'bite-sized' progression options within qualifications themselves.
>
> Source: *FLT: 14–19 Delivery Guidance for 2009/10*, LSC (August 2009)

For the pilot there were four defined Progression Pathways within FL (a first full Level 2; skilled work or an apprenticeship; supported employment or independent living; and appropriate provision for learners aged 14–19). This structure is under review based on the experience from the pilots, and the term Progression Pathways has been replaced by destination-led Personalised Learning Programmes.

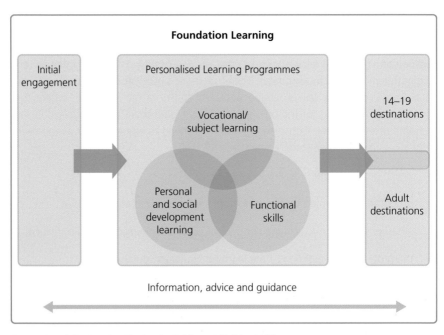

Source: *Foundation Learning Tier: Interim Guidance*, LSC (May 2009)

Funding FL Personalised Learning Programmes

FL qualifications and programmes are funded through the LSC's standard demand-led funding formula. The QCF qualifications (*see page 22*) that are eligible to support FL programmes are currently listed in the Foundation Learning Qualification Catalogue. This is available from the Qualifications and Curriculum Development Agency (QCDA) website at www.qcda.gov.uk/flt

The table below contains the qualifications and funding for an example FL programme. The Foundation Learning Qualification Catalogue not only contains the eligible FL qualifications, it also sets the rules of combination.

Progression to skilled work or an apprenticeship	SLN glh	SLN	Unweighted funding
Vocational learning			
Cert in Business Administration (L1)	105	0.233	£681
Award in Computerised Accounts (L1)	30	0.067	£195
Award in Business Finance (L1)	30	0.067	£195
Personal and Social Development learning (PSD)			
Cert in Employability and Personal Development (L1)	108	0.24	£701
Functional skills (*see page 90*)			
Award in English (L1)	36	0.08	£234
Award in Mathematics (L1)	36	0.08	£234
Award in ICT (L1)	36	0.08	£234
Entitlement, only eligible if programme is 336glh or more (*see page 68*)			
Entitlement	114	0.253	£740
Total	495	1.1	£3212

> **Note**
>
> As a transitional measure, during 2009/10 only, FL programmes can also be funded within the weekly funding methodology for Entry to Employment (*see page 88*). In this scenario, no further funding for qualifications, entitlement (*see page 68*) or additional learning support (*see page 44*) can be claimed.

14–19 Diploma

As part of the ongoing 14–19 qualification reform programme, the Department for Children, Schools and Families (DCSF), the Qualifications and Curriculum Authority (QCA), the Skills for Business Network (SfBN) and awarding bodies such as Edexcel have developed the new Diploma qualification. The QCA (now QCDA) describes the Diploma as being 'about learning a range of widely applicable skills and knowledge, set within a specialised context – a specified group of sectors and subjects'.

The Diploma programmes are available at Levels 1, 2 and 3.

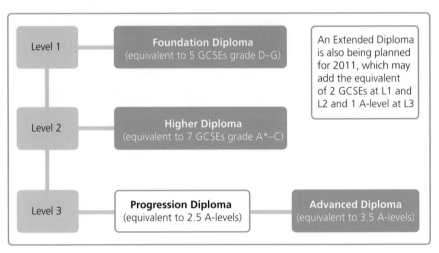

Providers need to be separately approved to deliver each line of learning, and there is a strong emphasis on working in partnership with other providers to deliver the programme.

The Diploma catalogues contain all the principal learning and project qualifications that are available to learners at each level, as well as a full listing of the functional skills and additional specialist learning options relevant to a specific line of learning. The Diploma catalogues can be accessed from the online National Database of Accredited Qualifications (NDAQ) at www.accreditedqualifications.org.uk and advice on curriculum and specification issues is available from www.qcda.gov.uk/5396.aspx

Provider collaboration

In many cases 16–18-year-old learners studying a 14–19 Diploma will be attending a number of providers within a consortium. One of the providers will be designated as the home provider, and it will be through them that funding is allocated and calculated (*see page 73*). Annex B of the LSC's 2009/10 *Funding Guidance Update* contains further details (*see page 15*).

The Diploma has a common structure, and at all levels balances practical and theoretical understanding within three components.

14–19 Diploma: common structure

Source: *The Diploma: an overview of the qualification*, QCA, Version 3 (2008)

Principal learning	Generic learning	Additional and specialist learning
50% applied learning	Work experience *Minimum 10 days*	
	Functional skills	
	Project	

Personal, learning and thinking skills

By 2010 there will be 14 vocational lines of learning, and a further three academic ones will be available from 2011. The 10 available in 2009/10 are listed below, along with the relevant programme weighting (applied only to the principal learning). To find out more about programme weightings *see page 34*.

Diploma lines available in 2009/10	Programme weighting	
	Level 1	Levels 2 & 3
Business, administration and finance	1.0 (A)	1.0 (A)
Construction and the built environment	1.3 (C)	1.3 (C)
Creative and media	1.3 (C)	1.3 (C)
Engineering	1.3 (C)	1.3 (C)
Environmental and land-based studies	1.6 (D)	1.6 (D)
Hair and beauty studies	1.3 (C)	1.3 (C)
Hospitality	1.3 (C)	1.3 (C)
Information technology	1.12 (B)	1.3 (C)
Manufacturing and product design	1.3 (C)	1.3 (C)
Society, health and development	1.12 (B)	1.12 (B)

Funding the 14–19 Diploma

Each component part of the Diploma has a standard learning number (SLN) value and funding is calculated separately for each component. Therefore, the learner would need to enrol on each element, although an overarching programme code within the individualised learner record (ILR) would link the elements together and determine whether the learner had passed or failed the Diploma. Functional skills, the project and the additional and specialist learning elements are also available for accreditation as separate learning aims in their own right.

The examples in this chapter apply the 2009/10 16–18 college national funding rate of £2920. However, a school sixth form would use the £3007 national funding rate (*see page 30*).

Foundation Diploma

The Foundation Diploma is at Level 1, and requires 600glh. It is the equivalent in terms of average length of study to five GCSEs and would normally be studied in one year if the learner was in post-compulsory education or two years if taken at the same time as the Key stage 4 National Curriculum programme of study.

Foundation Diploma: 600glh

Source: *The Diploma: an overview of the qualification*, QCA, Version 3 (2008)

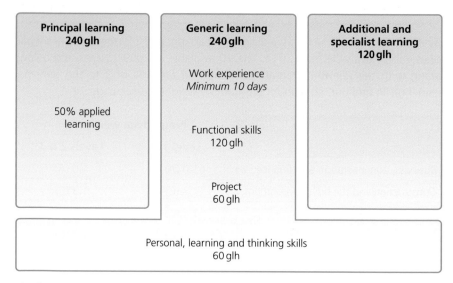

The funding rates for the Foundation Diploma include 30 SLN glh for the costs of collaboration.

Full-time 16–18-year-olds are also eligible for entitlement funding of 114 SLN glh (*see page 68*). In the example on the following page, the learner is enrolled on all three functional skills.

Foundation Diploma (Level 1)	SLN glh	SLN	Unweighted funding
Principal learning	240	0.533	£1557
Project	60	0.133	£389
Functional skills – English	36	0.08	£234
Functional skills – ICT	36	0.08	£234
Functional skills – mathematics	36	0.08	£234
Additional and specialist learning	120	0.267	£779
Personal learning & thinking skills	60	0.133	£389
Costs of collaboration	30	0.067	£195
Total (excl. entitlement)	**618**	**1.373**	**£4010**
16–18 entitlement	114	0.253	£740
Total (incl. entitlement)	**732**	**1.627**	**£4750**

Higher Diploma

The Higher Diploma is at Level 2, and requires 800 glh. It is the equivalent in terms of average length of study to seven GCSEs and would normally be studied in one or two years if the learner is in post-compulsory education, or two years if taken at the same time as the Key stage 4 National Curriculum programme of study.

Higher Diploma: 800 glh

Source: The Diploma: an overview of the qualification, QCA, Version 3 (2008)

Principal learning 420 glh	Generic learning 200 glh	Additional and specialist learning 180 glh
50% applied learning	Work experience *Minimum 10 days*	
	Functional skills 80 glh	
	Project 60 glh	

Personal, learning and thinking skills 60 glh

The funding rates for the Higher Diploma include 40 SLN glh for the costs of collaboration, may include entitlement funding (*see page 68*) and in the example below the learner is not enrolled on the functional skills in ICT (*see page 90*), as in this example it has already been attained.

Higher Diploma (Level 2)	SLN glh	SLN	Unweighted funding
Principal learning	420	0.933	£2725
Project	60	0.133	£389
Functional skills – English	36	0.08	£234
Functional skills – mathematics	36	0.08	£234
Additional and specialist learning	180	0.4	£1168
Personal learning & thinking skills	60	0.133	£389
Costs of collaboration	40	0.089	£260
Total (excl. entitlement)	**832**	**1.849**	**£5399**
16–18 entitlement (*see page 68*)	114	0.253	£740
Total (incl. entitlement)	**946**	**2.102**	**£6138**

As previously mentioned, a 16–18-year-old can study a Level 2 Higher Diploma over one year. The problem with this is that the 2.102 SLN exceeds the 1.75 SLN annual cap (*see page 29*). Therefore, if it were taught in one year funding would be reduced by 0.352 SLN (£1028). However, where the Level 2 Higher Diploma is delivered post-16 in one year, the costs of collaboration/work experience is funded outside the funding formula at a rate of £274 (in 2009/10 only).

> **Note**
>
> Selecting the most appropriate timetable and overall duration (one or two years) will be particularly important for Higher Diploma learners.

Advanced Diploma

The Advanced Diploma is at Level 3, and requires 1080 glh. It is the equivalent, in terms of the Universities and Colleges Admissions Service (UCAS) points, to 3.5 A-levels. It would normally be studied in post-compulsory education full-time over two years.

A minimum of Level 2 functional skills (English, mathematics and ICT) is required, although many will have already achieved this so they are not listed in the tables on the following page. Additional English, mathematics or ICT may be required at Level 3 for some lines of learning.

Advanced Diploma: 1080 glh

Source: The Diploma: an overview of the qualification, QCA, Version 3 (2008)

Principal learning 540 glh	Generic learning 180 glh	Additional and specialist learning 360 glh
50% applied learning	Work experience *Minimum 10 days* Extended project 120 glh	

Personal, learning and thinking skills 60 glh

Advanced Diploma (Level 3)	SLN glh	SLN	Unweighted funding
Principal learning	540	1.2	£3504
Extended project	120	0.267	£779
Additional and specialist learning	360	0.8	£2336
Personal learning & thinking skills	60	0.133	£389
Costs of collaboration	54	0.12	£350
Total	1134	2.52	£7358

There is also the option of a Progression Diploma at Level 3, which can be delivered completed in one year and is the equivalent to 2.5 A-levels.

Progression Diploma (Level 3)	SLN glh	SLN	Unweighted funding
Principal learning	540	1.2	£3504
Extended project	120	0.267	£779
Personal learning & thinking skills	60	0.133	£389
Costs of collaboration	36	0.08	£234
Total	756	1.68	£4906

BTEC qualifications

BTECs are unit- and portfolio-based work-related qualifications produced by Edexcel that have been around since 1984. In 2008 almost one and a half million young people and adults were enrolled on a BTEC course.

The BTEC Entry

BTEC Entry Certificates in Skills for Working Life and Life Skills either develop the initial skills for a broad work sector or confidence for everyday life. They are particularly popular for learners with learning difficulties or those who struggle with traditional learning. The funding rates are unlisted for these qualifications, so a 36-hour course for a 16-year-old in college would generate an unweighted funding of (36 / 450) × £2920 = £234.

BTEC Introductory

BTEC Introductory qualifications are at Level 1 and offer an entry point into an industry sector. The qualification model is composed of two qualifications, the four-unit Certificate and eight-unit Diploma. The Introductory Certificate is nested within the Introductory Diploma, which means the Certificate units are a sub-set of the Diploma. Providers can therefore deliver the Certificate, and then top-up to the Diploma by offering the additional four units required.

Edexcel recommends 180 glh for the Introductory Certificate and 360 glh for the Introductory Diploma, but the LSC analysed actual provider durations and have only listed the BTEC Introductory Diploma. This is because a common pattern of delivery could not be found for the BTEC Introductory Certificate, so the rate has been unlisted. This means that the rate is calculated using the provider glh (see page 28).

BTEC Introductory (Level 1)	SLN glh	SLN	Unweighted funding
BTEC Introductory Certificate	unlisted	glh / 450	SLN × £2920
BTEC Introductory Diploma	450	1	£2920

The graph below shows the listed and unlisted approach to unweighted funding for the BTEC Intoductory qualifications in colleges (assuming a maximum glh range of 100 to 300 for the Certificate and 300 to 500 for the Diploma).

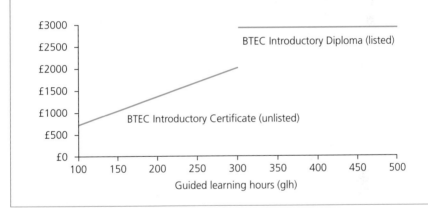

In most cases the SLN glh for the school sixth forms is the same as for colleges. However, the Introductory Certificate for schools has been listed at 225 SLN glh (and of course schools use a national funding rate of £3007).

The table below contains the unweighted funding for a BTEC Introductory Diploma programme funded at 16–18 college rates.

Example BTEC Introductory programme	SLN glh	SLN	Unweighted funding
BTEC Introductory Diploma	450	1	£2920
Key skills in communication	36	0.08	£234
Entitlement	114	0.253	£740
Total learner funding	600	1.333	£3893

BTEC First Certificate and Diploma

BTEC Firsts are at Level 2 and are the vocational equivalent of GCSE grades A*-C. They have traditionally been delivered in further education colleges. However, in recent years they have increasingly been delivered by schools, and they are currently the UK's fastest growing qualification.

There are over 60 BTEC Firsts, each linked to an industry sector, and for each BTEC First there are two qualifications; the three-unit First Certificate and the six-unit First Diploma. The First Certificate is nested within the First Diploma. Providers can therefore deliver the Certificate, in the first instance, and then once this has been achieved the learner can progress to the First Diploma.

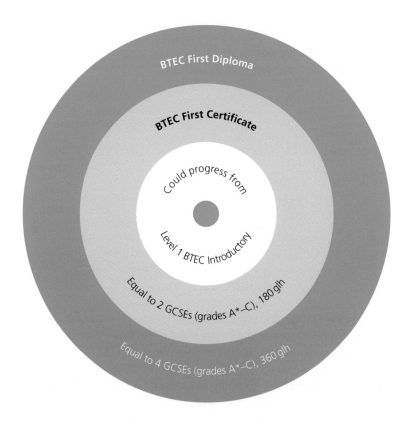

The Level 2 BTEC Firsts and the Level 3 BTEC Nationals (*see page 86*) are being redeveloped for accreditation on to the QCF for teaching from 1 September 2010 (*see page 22*). Edexcel has submitted over 120 titles to the regulator for accreditation. Structures and units can be found on the Edexcel website at www.edexcel.com/2010btecfirsts and www.edexcel.com/2010btecnationals

The First Diploma learner-responsive SLN value for colleges is the same as for school sixth forms, while the First Certificate rate is unlisted.

BTEC Firsts (Level 2)	SLN glh	SLN	Unweighted funding
BTEC First Certificate	unlisted	glh / 450	SLN × £2920
BTEC First Diploma	450	1	£2920

The graph below shows the listed and unlisted approach to unweighted funding for the BTEC Firsts in colleges (assuming a maximum glh range of 100 to 300 for the Certificate and 300 to 500 for the Diploma).

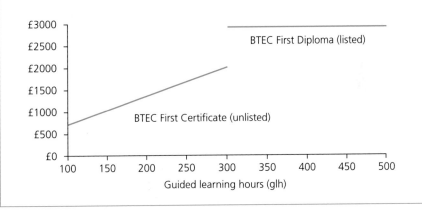

Note

To avoid claiming too much funding, the LSC have created conversion learning aims for progressions from a First Certificate to a Diploma.

Supplementary information about BTEC Firsts:
- BTEC First Diplomas exceed the 325 glh threshold (excluding NVQs) for a full Level 2. Therefore, first full Level 2 learners that achieve the Diploma will contribute to the Government's full Level 2 Public Service Agreement (PSA) target. In funding terms this places the First Diploma into the high priority classification.
- Adult first full Level 2 learners enrolled on the Diploma would be fee-remitted as part of the Level 2 entitlement. The First Diploma is also eligible for funding under the Train to Gain scheme (*see page 127*).
- Some BTEC Firsts are technical certificates within apprenticeship frameworks. For example, the BTEC First Diploma in Engineering is one of the options within the Level 2 Engineering Apprenticeship.

BTEC National Award, Certificate and Diploma

The Level 3 BTEC Nationals have for nearly 25 years been the vocational equivalent of A-levels in colleges, and in recent years have also increasingly been delivered by school sixth forms. There are over 250 BTEC Nationals; they are portfolio based and as nested qualifications they consist of Awards, Certificates and Diplomas within a single framework.

In terms of funding the BTEC Nationals, the LSC considered average provider delivery patterns, and for 2009/10 have kept the rates for the six-unit Award and 12-unit Certificate above the awarding body recommended guided learning hours (glh). However, in 2008/09 the LSC reduced funding for the 18-unit Diploma from the equivalent of 1440 glh down to 1080 glh.

BTEC Nationals (Level 3)	SLN glh	SLN	Unweighted funding
BTEC National Award	450	1	£2920
BTEC National Certificate	900	2	£5840
BTEC National Diploma	1080	2.4	£7008

As these are nested qualifications, learners achieving the BTEC National Award can study the additional units to achieve the Certificate or Diploma. The LSC have created learning aim conversion codes in order to fund this.

BTEC Nationals (Level 3)	SLN glh	SLN	Unweighted funding
Conversion from Award to Diploma	630	1.4	£4088
Conversion from Award to Certificate	450	1	£2920
Conversion from Certificate to Diploma	180	0.4	£1168

The 16–18-year-old funding for a two-year BTEC National Diploma is likely to include key skills and entitlement for tutorials and enrichment activities. Therefore, funding would be as follows (excluding 2010/11 inflation).

BTEC Nationals (Level 3)	SLN glh	SLN	Unweighted funding
BTEC National Diploma	1080	2.4	£7008
1 key skill over 2 years	228	0.507	£1479
Entitlement (2 years)	36	0.08	£234
Total learner (over 2 years)	1344	2.987	£8721

BTEC National Certificates and Diplomas are full Level 3 qualifications as they exceed the current 595glh threshold (excluding NVQs) for fullness at Level 3. Therefore, first full Level 3 learners that achieve would count towards the Government's Public Service Agreement (PSA) target. First full Level 3 adult learners under the age of 25 would also be eligible for fee remission via the Level 3 entitlement.

The BTEC Foundation Diploma in Art and Design is also at Level 3, and in 2007/08 grew to nine units and became a full Level 3. The awarding body glh is 600, although it will be funded in 2009/10 at 645 SLN glh (1.433 SLN). This generates unweighted 16–18 college funding of £4185.

Note

The 18-unit BTEC National Diploma is funded at the same rate as the 18-unit OCR Level 3 National Extended Diploma. The 12-unit BTEC National Certificate is funded at the same rate as the 12-unit OCR Level 3 National Diploma. Finally, the six-unit BTEC National Award is funded at the same rate as the six-unit OCR Level 3 National Certificate.

Entry to Employment

Entry to Employment (E2E) is a learning programme that has been available to 16–18-year-olds since 2003/04. E2E is designed to reduce the number of young people not in education, employment or training (NEET) by preparing them for progression to employment, further education or an apprenticeship. E2E provides the opportunity for greater flexibility than more traditional 16–18-year-old programmes as it is not time-bound, specified in terms of guided learning hours, nor qualification-driven (although qualifications will be appropriate and an incentive for some E2E learners). The duration, content and hours per week is based on the needs of each learner and funding will continue to be based on the number of weeks of learning attendance (as at midnight on the Monday of the week).

E2E funding has in the past been claimed by colleges and training providers as part of a work-based learning (WBL) contract. However, from 2008/09 E2E became funded from within the 16–18 learner-responsive funding model. This means funding claims to the LSC are no longer monthly, although many of the funding characteristics remain unchanged. These include a weekly rate and basic or enhanced bonuses if the learner achieves a qualification and progresses.

New E2E SLN values for 2009/10.

Entry to Employment	SLN	Unweighted funding
Weekly rate*	0.037	£108
Basic bonus (for achievement or positive progression)	0.062	£181
Enhanced bonus (for achievement or positive progression)	0.126	£368

*Entitlement funding cannot be claimed as it is included in the weekly rate.

The funding is therefore heavily dependent on the number of weeks a learner is on-programme, rather than a listed rate for a particular qualification type or for the number of guided learning hours delivered.

Entry to Employment example	SLN	Unweighted funding
12 weeks on the BTEC Entry Level Certificate in Skills for Working Life	0.444	£1296
Basic achievement bonus	0.062	£181
Enhanced progression bonus	0.126	£368
Total	0.632	£1845

The use of standard learner numbers (SLNs) and the national funding rate (NFR) applies. However, some elements in the provider factor (PF) for E2E do not apply in the same way as for other learners in the 16–18 funding model.

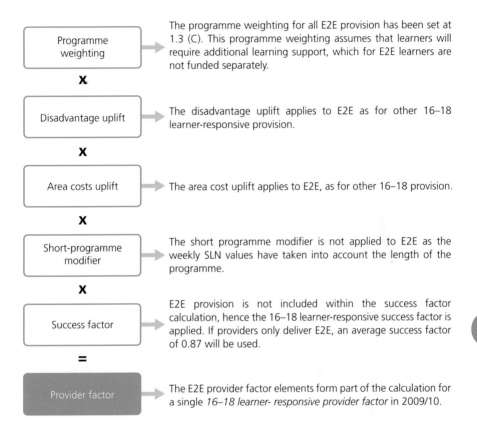

| Programme weighting | The programme weighting for all E2E provision has been set at 1.3 (C). This programme weighting assumes that learners will require additional learning support, which for E2E learners are not funded separately. |

X

| Disadvantage uplift | The disadvantage uplift applies to E2E as for other 16–18 learner-responsive provision. |

X

| Area costs uplift | The area cost uplift applies to E2E, as for other 16–18 provision. |

X

| Short-programme modifier | The short programme modifier is not applied to E2E as the weekly SLN values have taken into account the length of the programme. |

X

| Success factor | E2E provision is not included within the success factor calculation, hence the 16–18 learner-responsive success factor is applied. If providers only deliver E2E, an average success factor of 0.87 will be used. |

=

| Provider factor | The E2E provider factor elements form part of the calculation for a single *16–18 learner- responsive provider factor* in 2009/10. |

Hence the funding formula remains the same for E2E, with the exception of low-level ALS, which is funded within the programme weighting and SLN:

$$\text{SLN} \times \text{NFR} \times \text{PF} = \text{E2E funding}$$

Note

The 2009/10 LSC funding guidance states that for E2E 'it is expected that providers will be working towards the introduction of qualifications on the Qualifications and Credit Framework (QCF), in line with the Prospectus for Progression Pathways published by the LSC and QCA'. The QCF is explained in more detail on page 22 and the Progression Pathways, now called Personalised Learning Programmes, sit within Foundation Learning (*see page 74*).

Key and functional skills

Key skills qualifications

Key skills are primarily designed to be part of full-time 16–18 learner programmes or apprenticeship frameworks. There are six key skills qualifications (three standard and three wider key skills), and all are available from Level 1 through to Level 4.

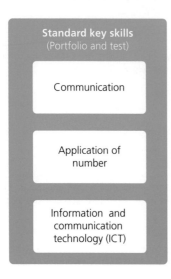

Standard key skills
(Portfolio and test)

- Communication
- Application of number
- Information and communication technology (ICT)

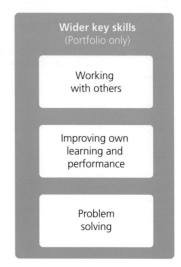

Wider key skills
(Portfolio only)

- Working with others
- Improving own learning and performance
- Problem solving

Key skills funding

The standard key skills funding rate across all funding models and at all levels is listed at 36 SLN glh, whilst wider key skills in the learner-responsive models (with the exception of school sixth forms), are unlisted.

Key skills	SLN glh	SLN	Unweighted funding
Standard	36	0.08	£234
Wider	unlisted	glh / 450	SLN × £2920

Key skills are usually taught as part of the 16–18 entitlement (see page 68) and since 2008/09 each qualification has been funded separately.

> **Note**
>
> Key skills in communication and application of number at Level 1 and Level 2 contribute to the Government's numeracy and literacy Public Service Agreement (PSA) target. In line with other basic skills qualifications they also have a programme weighting of 1.4 (F).

Functional skills qualifications

Functional skills are practical skills in English, mathematics and information and communication technology (ICT). The pilot for functional skills qualifications began in September 2007 and by September 2010 they will replace all the key skills qualifications. During the pilot they are available as free-standing qualifications at Entry Level, Level 1 and Level 2. Functional skills are five credit Awards on the Qualifications and Credit Framework (*see page 22*).

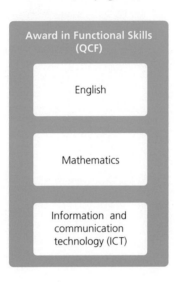

Functional skills qualifications feature within each of the four qualification routes for 14–19 year olds (GCSEs, Diplomas, apprenticeships and Foundation Learning). For example, all apprenticeship frameworks will require English and mathematics functional skills, most will also require ICT.

Functional skills funding

During the pilot phase the SLN rates for colleges are unlisted, which means the funding is dependent on the provider glh. This allows the LSC to fund and monitor the rate based on actual duration before determining the most appropriate listed rate for 2010/11. However, school sixth forms do not have the option of unlisted rates, so the LSC have applied the same listed rate used for key skills, 36 SLN glh.

Functional skills	SLN glh	SLN	Unweighted funding
Colleges	unlisted	glh / 450	SLN × £2920
School sixth forms	36	0.08	£234

Functional skills in English and mathematics have a programme weighting of 1.4 (F), whilst ICT has a programme weighting of 1.12 (B) (*see page 34*).

Adult college funding

This chapter includes a number of qualifications that are delivered to adults through the adult learner-responsive (ALR) funding model (*see page 18*).

The range of ALR providers

The great majority of ALR funding is allocated to Further Education (FE) colleges, hence the name of this chapter. However, there are a number of other providers who deliver ALR funded provision, such as higher education institutions and local authorities.

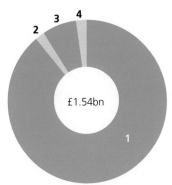

08/09 ALR allocations
Source: *LSC Allocations Spreadsheet*

1. FE colleges (89%)

2. HE institutions (2%)

3. Local authorities (7%)

4. Other public and private organisations (2%)

The majority of FE colleges with ALR allocations are general or tertiary colleges. However, there are a number of other types of colleges.

08/09 FE College ALR allocations
Source: *LSC Allocations Spreadsheet*

1. General FE colleges including tertiary (93%)

2. Sixth form colleges (2%)

3. Special colleges (agriculture, art etc) (2%)

4. Specialist designated colleges (3%)

Every provider with an ALR allocation, regardless of type, is funded using the demand-led funding formula (*see page 27*).

The range of ALR provision

This chapter contains examples of qualifications and units which can be ALR-funded. With the exception of entitlement (*see page 68*) and Entry to Employment (*see page 88*), qualifications within the school sixth form and 16–18 college funding chapters can be also funded under the ALR funding model (including Foundation Learning). However, it is important to use the ALR funding formula elements, such as the national funding rate of £2817. Also, adults may be ineligible for fee remission (*see page 52*).

ALR eligibility, formula, rates and reconciliation

To access ALR funding in 2009/10 a learner must be 19 or over on 31 August 2009 and satisfy the LSC learner eligibility requirements (*see page 50*). Learners who are 19 on 31 August but who started their course in 2008/09 (when they were 18) are funded at 16–18 rates but contribute to ALR targets and generate funding from the ALR allocation.

The qualifications and courses which are eligible for ALR funding are determined by the LSC, and can be found within the Learning Aim Database (*see page 138*). As outlined on page 18, the majority of ALR funding allocations have reduced in 2009/10, and the remaining ALR funding has shifted towards PSA target-bearing provision (*see page 13*).

Funding formula

ALR funding applies the same demand-led funding formula used in schools and for 16–18 provision in colleges, but at ALR rates (*see page 27*).

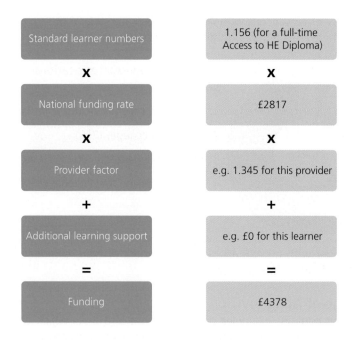

Standard learner numbers	1.156 (for a full-time Access to HE Diploma)
X	X
National funding rate	£2817
X	X
Provider factor	e.g. 1.345 for this provider
+	+
Additional learning support	e.g. £0 for this learner
=	=
Funding	£4378

The provision within this chapter includes examples of unweighted funding. This means the SLN value has only been multiplied by the national funding rate. Thus, for ALR funding in 2009/10 the unweighted funding would be the SLN multiplied by £2817. The same principle applies for 16–18 provision in schools (£3007) and 16–18 learner-responsive provision in colleges (£2920).

Rates

As outlined on page 28, where a qualification rate (SLN glh) is listed on the Learning Aim Database it is divided by 450 to determine the SLN value. A-levels and GCSEs have a day and evening rate (*see pages 62 and 64*). When the Learning Aim Database does not have a listed rate, the size of the provider's programme (glh) is divided by 450 to calculate the SLN value. Each learner programme has an annualised SLN cap of 1.75. The unweighted funding in 2009/10 is calculated as SLN × £2817.

Reconciliation

ALR funding is paid to providers in monthly instalments based on a national profile. However, ALR funding is neither plan-led (paid for the plan) like 16–18 provision, nor truly demand-led (only paid for actual delivery) like employer-responsive provision. This is because there are mid-year and year-end reconciliation rules, with tolerances, to reduce or clawback funding from underperforming providers. These rules are also used to increase allocations or payments for over-performing providers (subject to funds being made available from under-performing ALR providers).

The reconciliation rules changed during 2008/09, and the tolerence for clawback was increased from 3% to 5%. However, the rules for 2009/10 have reverted back to the original rules published for 2008/09. This means if a provider delivers less than 97% of their SLNs by the end of the academic year, they will only receive 97% of their allocation (3% clawback).

Reconciliation rules		
Source: *Funding Guidance 2009/10 Update v4.0*, LSC (July 2009)		
Tolerance for growth	Mid-year and final	5%
Tolerance for clawback	Mid-year	5%
	Final	3%
Maximum growth (cap)	Mid-year	108% (3% payable)
	Final	108% (3% payable)*
Maximum clawback (cap)	Mid-year	95% of allocation
	Final	97% of allocation

*This figure may rise after mid-year claims are received and processed. Payment of growth is subject to affordability.

The LSC had considered options for virement of funding from one funding model to another during 2009/10, which would have had implications on the reconciliation rules. Providers should regularly check the LSC website for any further funding updates. Also, from April 2010 the Skills Funding Agency (SFA) will take responsibility from the LSC for ALR funding.

Adult Numeracy and Literacy

There are a number of numeracy and literacy qualifications which sit within the umbrella term Skills for Life, including key skills and GCSEs in English and mathematics. In the adult sector, there are two qualifications available at five levels, the Certificate in Adult Numeracy and Certificate in Adult Literacy.

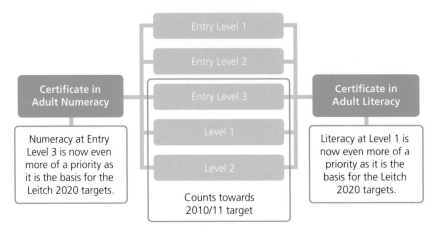

The level at which the learner achieves the qualification determines whether it contributes to the government target and there are a number of funding traits which are shared by all these certificates:

- learners are automatically eligible for fee remission and are therefore fully-funded;
- they carry a basic skills programme weighting of 1.4 (F) in the learner- and employer-responsive models (*see page 34*);
- basic skills learners, as defined by the LSC, have a 1.12 disadvantage uplift in the learner-responsive funding model (*see page 36*);
- the funding rates are unlisted in the learner-responsive model and listed in the employer-responsive model (*see page 28*).

Unweighted and unlisted adult funding 2009/10

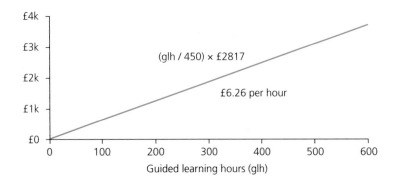

The funding rates for Certificates in Adult Numeracy and Literacy qualifications within the employer-responsive funding model are listed at 0.193 SLN (see *Train to Gain section on page 127*).

Supplementary information about literacy and numeracy and basic skills provision (including ESOL):

- GCSEs in English and mathematics at grades D-G contribute to Skills for Life targets at Level 1, and grades A*-C at Level 2. However, they are not classed as basic skills qualifications, so attract neither a programme weighting of 1.4 nor automatic fee remission.

- A two-year pilot of new functional skills qualifications started in September 2007 (*see page 90*), and it is anticipated they will replace the main key skills qualifications and Certificates in Adult Literacy and Numeracy from 2010/11 (*see page 91*).

- Providers can claim funding for non-approved basic skills provision which is not on the National Qualifications Framework, such as at pre-Entry Level. However, claims for non-approved Level 1 and 2 basic skills provision are discouraged and it is no longer part of the Skills for Life offer. As such it attracts neither a programme weighting of 1.4 nor automatic fee remission for basic skills enrolments.

- The *LSC Grant Letter 2009–10* states that the volume of Skills for Life learners is planned to increase by 3% in the adult learner-responsive funding model and by 7% in the employer-responsive funding model. To achieve the ambitious Skills for Life targets the expectation is that providers will reduce non-approved and low-level approved non-target-bearing Skills for Life in favour of target-bearing Skills for Life (particularly numeracy, for which there is a national marketing campaign).

- From 2006/07 the LSC stopped funding short three- and six-hour Skills for Life diagnostics and taster sessions via further education funding.

- Learners on a numeracy or literacy basic skills enrolment should not be charged tuition fees nor any other costs directly relating to their enrolment. Additional non-basic skills enrolments would not be eligible for remission funding and the learner would normally pay a fee (unless the learner is otherwise eligible for fee remission). The LSC no longer funds candidates to take stand-alone Skills for Life tests; providers can charge a fee for this service.

- Learners on a numeracy or literacy course are not eligible for additional learning support (ALS) funding if the intention is to use it to further support their numeracy and literacy skills.

English for Speakers of Other Languages

LSC-funded courses in English for Speakers of Other Languages (ESOL) sit within the umbrella term Skills for Life and are for learners who require language skills to perform the necessities of daily life. ESOL, unlike English as a Foreign Language (EFL), is supported by the Government in an effort to help people settle into their adopted country.

The main ESOL qualification is the Certificate in ESOL Skills for Life, which is available at five levels and contains three mandatory units at each level.

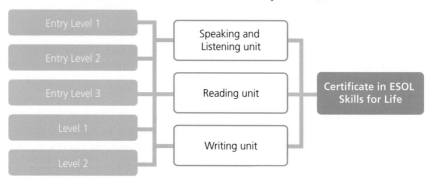

Individual units can be funded separately, but until the learner achieves the full certificate they cannot contribute to the Government's Skills for Life targets (Entry Level 3 and above for the original target and Level 1 for the Leitch target). Learners who achieve the various units at different levels are known as having a spiky profile. Once all three units have been achieved the full certificate is awarded at the lowest level.

Certificate in ESOL Skills for Life: spiky profile example

The basic skills programme weighting of 1.4 and disadvantage uplift of 1.12 are funded in the same way as for the Certificate in Adult Numeracy and Literacy. However, in 2007/08 automatic fee remission for ESOL enrolments was removed. This means that unless learners are eligible for fee remission (such as being on income-related benefits) a fee element is deducted from the funding (*see page 52*).

Funding rates for ESOL Skills for Life units and qualifications within the learner-responsive funding models are generally unlisted. This means the funding rate is based on the provider glh (as described in the formula chapter). The graph below shows that the unweighted funding per glh is £6.26 for the fully funded learner and £3.29 for fee-paying co-funded learners. Therefore £2.97 has been deducted as the fee element.

Adult learner-responsive ESOL Skills for Life funding (unweighted)

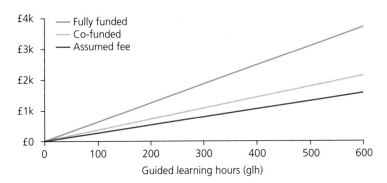

The funding rates for ESOL qualifications within the employer-responsive funding model are listed at 0.18 SLN (*see page 127*).

Certificate in ESOL for Work
Following the Government's review of ESOL provision in 2006 a new suite of ESOL for Work (EfW) qualifications was introduced in August 2007. These qualifications have been developed to 'support a shorter, more job-focused, practical approach to English language skills'. EfW qualifications are not part of Skills for Life and therefore do not contribute to government targets nor attract a programme weighting of 1.4 or disadvantage uplift of 1.12 within the learner-responsive funding formula. The LSC have listed the EfW qualification rate at 150 SLN glh, and given that most learners will be in work, it will generate the lower co-funding.

ESOL for Work	SLN glh	SLN	Co-funding (unweighted)	Assumed fee
Entry 3 & Level 1	150	0.333	£493	£446

Certificate in ESOL International
The international ESOL qualifications are different from EfW as they are 'intended primarily for the overseas market and for those who want or need an internationally recognised qualification'. They are not eligible for LSC funding nor do they contribute to government targets. This includes the International English Language Testing System (IELTS).

Access to HE Diploma

Access to HE qualifications were established in the 1970s, and in 2008/09 a newly validated Access to HE Diploma was launched. These qualifications are specially designed to prepare adult learners for entry into higher education by providing the underpinning knowledge and skills needed to progress to a degree or diploma course. As such, they are Level 3 qualifications which generally provide adults with a one-year alternative to the traditional two-year A-level pathway.

Access to HE Diplomas are available at most further education colleges, in a wide range of subjects. Approximately 20,000 Access to HE learners apply to universities each year. One of the interesting features of these qualifications is that they are neither part of the National Qualifications Framework (NQF) nor regulated by the Qualifications and Curriculum Authority (QCA). The approval of Access to HE courses is in fact managed by the universities' own quality assurance organisation, the Quality Assurance Agency for Higher Education (QAA).

SLN values for Access to HE qualifications within the adult learner-responsive funding model are the same as the rates for National Vocational Qualifications (NVQs) (*see page 102*). There is a listed value for enrolments of 450 glh and above (full-time) and an unlisted value for enrolments below 450 glh (part-time).

Access to HE	SLN glh	SLN	Unweighted funding
450 glh or more	520	1.156	£3255
Less than 450 glh	Provider glh	glh / 450	SLN × £2817

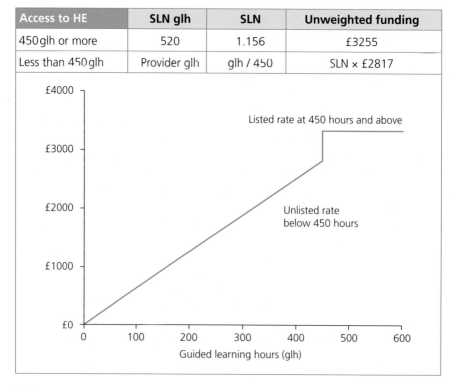

If the learner were ineligible for fee remission, 47.5% of the unweighted funding would be deducted as the fee element (also known as the assumed fee) (*see page 52*).

Access to HE assumed fee	Full-time	Part-time
Access to HE	£1546	SLN × £2817 × 47.5%

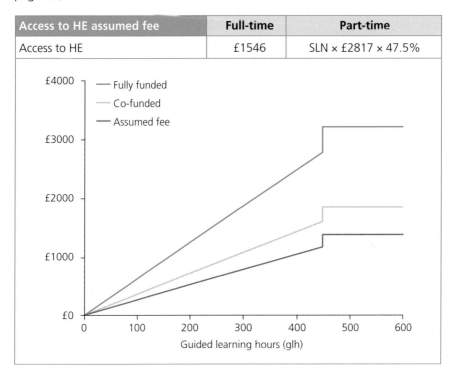

Supplementary information about Access to HE:

- Access to HE Diplomas are classified as full Level 3 courses even though they are neither on the NQF nor above the 595 glh threshold (excluding NVQs) for a full Level 3 qualification. This means that a first full Level 3 learner who achieves the qualification would contribute to the Department for Business Innovation and Skills (BIS) Public Service Agreement (PSA) target at Level 3. It is also specifically designed to progress learners into HE, and participation in HE is a PSA target for the DCSF (*see page 13*).
- As a contributor to PSA targets in two government departments, Access to HE is a high-priority qualification. This is of course maintained only when a sufficient percentage of learners are achieving the qualification, and preferably progressing into higher education.
- As a full Level 3 qualification, first full Level 3 learners under the age of 25 would be eligible for fee remission via the Level 3 entitlement. Some adults enrolled to an Access to HE Diploma would be first full Level 2 learners, in which case as 'jumpers' they would be eligible to remission at any age via the Level 2 entitlement.
- LSC funding for Access to HE in 2007/08 was approximately £70m.

National Vocational Qualifications

National Vocational Qualifications (NVQs) are work-related, competence-based qualifications that are achieved through assessment and training.

NVQs are a mandatory component of the apprenticeship framework, but they can also be delivered on the provider's premises on a full-time basis or for employers as part-time day or block release. Increasingly they are also being delivered as stand-alone work-based qualifications on the employer's premises (usually as part of the Train to Gain programme). In funding terms this makes the NVQ a relatively complex qualification, as they have listed and unlisted rates and can be funded from any one of the three funding models. The SLN rates are listed on the LAD (*see page 138*).

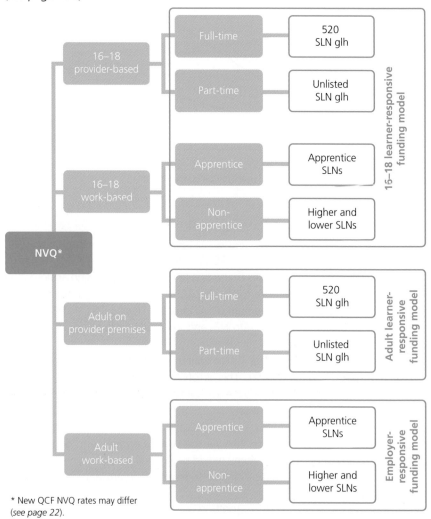

* New QCF NVQ rates may differ
(*see page 22*).

The SLN value for NVQs within the adult learner-responsive funding model is the same as the rates for Access to HE Diplomas (*see page 100*). There is a listed value for enrolments of 450 glh and above (full-time) and an unlisted value for enrolments below 450 glh (part-time).

NVQs (adult learner-responsive)	SLN glh	SLN	Unweighted funding
450 glh or more	520	1.156	£3255
Less than 450 glh	Provider glh	glh / 450	SLN × £2817

Guided learning hours (glh)

Listed rate at 450 hours and above

Unlisted rate below 450 hours

Supplementary information about NVQs:
- By 2010/11 all NVQs will need to fit within the QCF. This is likely to have a significant impact on the way the qualifications are marketed, delivered and assessed (*see page 22*).
- The SLN value and programme weighting for NVQs can differ for each funding model, and between apprenticeships and Train to Gain. Within the apprenticeship model the NVQ SLN is higher than for Train to Gain as it also includes an 'apprenticeship element'. In future the apprenticeship element may be funded separately.

Note

All Level 2 and 3 NVQs are currently full, which means learners may contribute to the Government's PSA targets. Also, first full Level 2 adults are fully-funded, with the exception of 19+ apprenticeships (*see page 122*).

Unit funding trials

The unit funding trials within the adult learner-responsive funding model began on 2 January 2009 and will continue in 2009/10.

The key objective will be to test whether unit funding can incentivise the completion of full qualifications, supporting the achievement of Public Service Agreement (PSA) targets particularly among individuals who would not otherwise engage with learning, and progress to complete qualifications.

The trials will be **limited** to Qualifications and Credit Framework (QCF) provision **only** and will also support the testing of a **Credit Success Rate** (CSR) measure to track learner progression to full qualifications. In addition, the trial will test how the technical features of the QCF, in particular the rules of combination, and the requirement for a Unique Learner Number (ULN) can be used to ensure providers support learners to progress from units for engagement to full qualifications.

Source: *Unit Funding Trials 2008/09 – 2009/10*, LSC (December 2008)

Provider eligibility

Any provider with an adult learner-responsive funding allocation can participate in the trial. However, there is no new funding available and the trial should not displace funding from target-bearing provision (*see below*).

Budget implications

There is no new funding available in addition to the agreed provider allocations for 2009/10. For units of Level 2 and 3 qualifications, funding must be displaced from developmental learning, and for units of Entry and Level 1 provision within Personalised Learning Programmes, funding must be displaced from Foundation Learning. In other words, funding should not be displaced for the unit funding trial from Skills for Life or full Level 2 and 3 provision, as they contribute to PSA targets.

Unit eligibility

The adult learner-responsive model trial has been restricted to 583 QCF units. The eligible units are available in a spreadsheet from http://qfr.lsc.gov.uk/ukvqrp/support. Each unit has an eight-digit reference number, which is to be used instead of a learning aim. For example, R5013788 is the reference number for the Workplace Communication unit at Level 2. The SLN glh and programme weighting for each unit is held within the Learning Aim Database (*see page 138*). More information, such as the rules of combination, details of the credits within the relevant unit and the associated parent qualification are held on the National Database of Accredited Qualifications (NDAQ).

Unit funding

The unit trials are funded within the adult learner-responsive funding model, and as such the same demand-led funding formula applies (see page 27).

The tables below include two eligible units and their relevant programme weighted funding values in 2009/10. These two examples also helpfully demonstrate that within the QCF there is no direct link between the credit value, recommended glh or funded SLN glh (see page 22).

Managing the employment relationship (Level 3)	
Unit reference	R5013810
Credit value	2
Recommended glh	7
SLN glh	5 (so SLN of 0.011)
Programme weighting	A (1.0)
Programme weighted funding	£31

The Care of Dry Sows and Gilts (Level 2)	
Unit reference	T5010754
Credit value	7
Recommended glh	70
SLN glh	80 (so SLN of 0.178)
Programme weighting	E (1.72)
Programme weighted funding	£861

QCF units sit within larger Awards, Certificates and Diplomas, known as parent qualifications. It will be the responsibility of the provider to ensure that no learners are double funded if they progress onto a parent qualification. Double funding is avoided by using the relevant discount value within field A51a of the individualised learner record (see page 23).

Note

The Level 2 and 3 units are limited to 19+ learners. However, the trial may encompass learners aged 16 plus for Entry and Level 1 units.

Pre-employment

This is a new chapter for the 2009/10 edition of *The hands-on guide to post-16 funding* and covers four new funding streams. Two streams were created in direct response to the economic downturn (Response to Redundancy and the Six-month Offer), and all four are designed to deliver skills training that help individuals gain sustainable employment. Many providers, including colleges, will be working with Jobcentre Plus for the first time to deliver this pre-employment provision. The Government's ambition is that after the learner is supported into employment the progression will be seamless onto adult and employer-responsive provision.

Employability Skills Programme
The Employability Skills Programme (ESP) is the LSC's main programme for the delivery of basic literacy, language, numeracy and employability skills, and qualifications to Jobcentre Plus (JCP) customers. Unlike any other funding stream, maximum contract values come from the adult learner-responsive allocation but payment to providers is made via the monthly employer-responsive methodology. It is anticipated that a number of smaller employability programmes, such as Skills for Jobs, will be gradually wound down to make way for successor programmes like ESP.

Response to Redundancy
Response to Redundancy is an LSC-funded programme worth £100m, half funded from the European Social Fund (ESF) and half funded from Train to Gain (*see page 127*). It was one of the first initiatives that was introduced alongside a range of measures to tackle the economic downturn and rising unemployment. Regional specifications vary, but all contracts use national funding rates, with a maximum of £1500 per learner. Funding is available from April 2009 to December 2010.

Six-month Offer
The £83m for the Sixth-month Offer was announced shortly after Response to Redundacy, and while similar it is only eligible for individuals unemployed for six months or more. It is also only available to providers with both adult-learner and employer-responsive contracts. This means that it was generally only colleges that were awarded contracts. The national funding rates are the same as for Response to Redundancy. Funding is available from April 2009 to July 2010.

Flexible New Deal
The Flexible New Deal (FND) is a Department for Work and Pensions (DWP) programme, specifically designed to support the longer-term unemployed (12 months plus) for a period of up to 52 weeks. In October 2009 it replaces a number of the existing New Deal programmes. The DWP expects to spend approximately £1.2 billion through the FND over the next five years. A small number of suppliers will hold large five-year contracts until 2016. However it is anticipated that much of the provision will be delivered by sub-contractors from the public, private and third sectors. Failure to participate in the programme could lead to individuals losing the Job Seekers Allowance (JSA).

Employability Skills Programme

The Employability Skills Programme (ESP) is the LSC's main programme for the delivery of basic literacy, language, numeracy and employability skills, and qualifications to Jobcentre Plus customers.

Eligible providers
It is primarily colleges that are eligible for ESP, as the funding is allocated through the adult learner-responsive budget (*see page 18*). However, uniquely, payment to providers is made via the employer-responsive methodology and system (*see page 20*). This means that the funding for ESP is based on monthly data returns and payments relate to actual rather than profiled delivery. ESP providers have been allocated a maximum contract value (MCV) from August 2009 to March 2010. Funding beyond March 2010 is dependent on provider performance and the total amount of funding that is made available for the 2010–11 financial year.

Eligible learners
All Jobcentre Plus customers aged 18 and above with an identified basic skills need are eligible for the programme.

Eligible provision
The following comprise fundable ESP elements:

- Approved basic skills qualifications at all levels up to and including Level 2. The LSC publish the list of these on their website.

- Approved employability qualifications at all levels up to and including Level 2. The LSC publish the list of these on their website.

- Full-time job outcomes (16 or more hours a week) started within 13 weeks of the end of the programme and that lasts for at least four weeks.

- Provision of an initial assessment, information, advice and guidance and referral that does not result in a programme start.

ESP funding formula
All qualifications delivered via ESP are funded with a national funding rate (NFR) of £2901, the same as Train to Gain (*see page 127*).

The funding formula for an ESP qualification is:

$$\text{Standard Learner Number (SLN)} \times \text{NFR} \times \text{weighting} = \pounds$$

Under the employer-responsive payment arrangements, 75% of the rate is payable on programme and 25% on outcome achievement (*see page 134*).

There is also additional funding available for the job outcome as well as a service fee where ESP provision is not pursued.

Qualification	SLN	NFR	Weighting	Funding
Basic skill	0.193	£2901	1.4	£784
Employability	0.178	£2901	1.5	£775

ESP funding values for 2009/10

In addition, providers can claim for a job outcome and non-starter service fee using a Training Provider Statement (TPS).

Other funded elements	Funding
Job outcome. Full-time job outcomes (16 or more hours a week) started within 13 weeks of the end of the programme and that lasts for at least four weeks.	£120
Non-starter service fee. For learners who do not pursue ESP provision, but are referred elsewhere to other/more appropriate provision, or have a start date but fail to start the programme.	£50

ESP planning assumptions
In the setting of provider MCVs the national LSC planning assumption is that they will average 2.37 qualifications with an achievement rate of 40%.

Other LSC-funded employability programmes
A number of other discrete LSC-funded employability programmes will continue into 2009/10.

One such programme is **Skills for Jobs**, which is primarily delivered by providers in London. Like ESP, the maximum funding per learner is £1500 and the target group is low-skilled adults, not currently in employment and who want to work. However, there is no requirement to deliver a qualification, and the £1500 funding is split three ways.

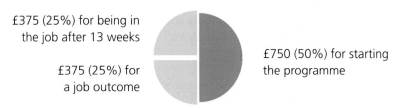

£375 (25%) for being in the job after 13 weeks

£375 (25%) for a job outcome

£750 (50%) for starting the programme

It is anticipated that programmes such as Skills for Jobs will be gradually wound-down to make way for successor programmes like ESP.

Response to Redundancy

In October 2008, the then Skills Secretary John Denham announced a package of measures in response to the economic downturn. As part of this package, the LSC was allocated £100m to support workers affected by redundancy. Of the £100m, half came from the European Social Fund (ESF) and the remaining half from the Train to Gain budget. The funding is available to providers from April 2009 until December 2010, with monitoring through to June 2011.

Aims of the £100m Response to Redundancy programme

The aim of this offer is to ensure that training provision is in place to enable providers to respond to redundancies and the employment implications of the present economic climate, and to fill gaps in mainstream LSC funding for individuals at risk of being made redundant or who have been made redundant.

Providers will be expected to develop working links with Jobcentre Plus in order to provide support and skills development activities that are relevant to both identified vacancies and forthcoming sectoral-based skills demand in local labour markets. The aim of providers must be to move people into employment in local labour markets with the realistic prospect of them progressing in work through further training, and to continue to support individuals once in the work force through the employer-responsive funding stream.

Source: £100m *Response to Redundancy Pre-employment training programme guidance for providers*, LSC (April 2009)

Eligible providers

The LSC published the specification and regional requirements for Response to Redundancy in January 2009, which invited tenders to be submitted in early March for programmes beginning in April. Tenders were encouraged from colleges and private training providers with employer-responsive contracts (*see page 20*), so that learners could seamlessly progress onto Train to Gain (*see page 127*) or apprenticeship (*see page 117*) programmes.

Eligible learners

The Response to Redundancy programme is for individuals aged 18 or over who would be eligible for LSC and ESF funding under normal rules. They also need to fall into one of the three following categories:

1. those under notice of redundancy
2. the newly unemployed
3. the longer-term unemployed who are job ready.

However, not all contracts include provision for all three categories. In general this is determined by the regional specification (*see page 14*).

Response to Redundancy package

The LSC state that the total package funded through the Response to Redundancy programme will typically be between two weeks full-time and/or eight weeks part-time. This timeframe ensures Jobcentre Plus regulations are adhered to in terms of attending full-time training and availability for work. Helping learners refresh their skills in a sector or begin the work of retraining for new skills to aid progression into employment is expected to be the key driver of any activity.

Providers are expected to offer the following range of skills interventions tailored to the needs of the individual (not all needed in each case).
- Training needs analysis and individual learning plan.
- Skills for Life diagnostic (including ICT) and delivery of appropriate training.
- Assessment of generic employability skills needs and the delivery of training to improve job search, job application and in-work skills.
- Information and advice and learner support.
- Training to update skills needed for a specific employment sector.
- Pre-employment training to provide skills to enter a different occupation or sector.
- Regular progress reviews.
- Exit interviews and customer tracking.

Providers need not offer qualifications, but where accreditation, including units, is available, this should be considered.

Response to Redundancy funding

Funding is available up to a maximum of £1500 per learner. The national funding formula, based on the delivery of guided learner hours (glh) within bandwidths, is as follows:

Funding for delivery based on glh and production of an individualised learning plan	Funding
Between 9 and 14 glh	£270
15–44 glh	£500
45–74 glh	£850
75 glh or more	£1200
Successful job start outcome **and** progression into further workplace training, such as an apprenticeship	£300

An initial payment of £200 is triggered once the first nine hours of training in any glh bandwidth have been delivered.

Six-month Offer

At an employment summit in January 2009 the Prime Minister announced a package of four measures aimed at ensuring individuals reaching six months of unemployment are offered continuing and relevant support to get back into work.

1. A **recruitment and training subsidy** of up to £2500 for companies that take on new recruits (£1000 recruitment subsidy and typically £1500 of training through Train to Gain once in work (*see page 127*).

2. A **self-employment package**, developed by the Department for Work and Pensions (DWP) and Department for Business Enterprise and Regulatory Reform (BERR) – now BIS – on an enhanced offer via Jobcentre Plus and Business Link.

3. A new approach to **volunteering**, which will be supported by specialist brokers.

4. A **new training package** allocated £83m of LSC funding, called the Six-month Offer, which is 'tailored support for those whose skills levels have proved to be a barrier to a quick entry into employment'. The £83m is being distributed over a 16-month period from April 2009 to July 2010.

The £83m Six-month Offer
The LSC state that 'it is important that this offer provides a distinctive and substantial level of support both to avoid duplicating other offers and to deliver a significant impact on an individual's chances of achieving a sustainable job and longer-term career progression'.

Example fit with other provision
Source: *Skills provision for those reaching six months' unemployed delivery plan v3.0*, LSC (May 2009)

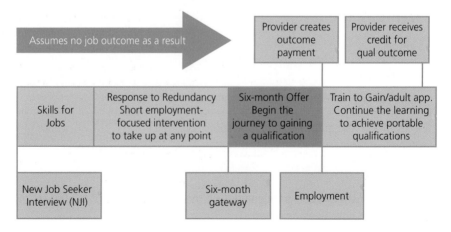

Eligible providers

Only those colleges in receipt of adult learner-responsive funding (ALR) (*see page 18*) and employer-responsive funding (ER) (*see page 20*) are eligible. This is because the LSC expect providers to progress learners from the Six-month Offer to one of their ALR or ER programmes.

Eligible learners

The Six-month Offer training programme is available to individuals claiming Jobseekers Allowance (JSA) who have been unemployed for six months or longer from April 2009. Candidates could be identified by Jobcentre Plus, by next-step advisers or by colleges directly recruiting.

Sixth-month Offer funding

As with Response to Redundancy (*see page 110*), funding is available up to a maximum of £1500 per learner. The national funding formula, based on the delivery of guided learner hours (glh) within bandwidths, is as follows:

Funding for delivery based on glh and production of an Individual Learning Plan	Funding
Between 9 and 14 glh	£270
15–44 glh	£500
45–74 glh	£850
75 glh or more	£1200
Successful job start outcome **and** evidence of ongoing learning towards a full Level 2 or full Level 3	£300

An initial payment of £200 is triggered once the first nine hours of training in any glh bandwidth have been delivered.

Most learners on the £83m 'training offer for people unemployed for over six months' will be eligible for wider fee remission and will not be charged tuition fees when transferring onto adult learner-responsive provision to complete their programme of learning. For those who would not otherwise be eligible, providers will be able to claim fee remission for them for the whole of the academic year in those cases where providers are also reducing funding through field A51a because of the learners' prior attendance on the Six-month Offer. Otherwise learners are only eligible for fee remission for adult learner-responsive provision where they meet the standard fee remission guidance. As is normal practice, for learners who continue with their learning, providers should establish eligibility for fee remission at the start of the next academic year.

Source: *Funding Guidance 2009/10 v4.0*, LSC (July 2009)

Flexible New Deal

The Flexible New Deal (FND) is funded by the Department for Work and Pensions (DWP), and has been included within this book as it will be the largest source of funding for providers delivering training and support to the long-term unemployed. The DWP expects to spend approximately £1.2 billion through the FND over the next five years.

New Deal history

The original New Deal programme was introduced in 1998 to support those on Job Seekers Allowance (JSA) to find work. In 2007 the DWP published the Green Paper, *In work, better off: next steps to full employment*, followed shortly by the White Paper, *Ready for Work: full employment in our generation*. These papers described a new phase of welfare reform which included refreshing the JSA regime and modernising the New Deal to end long-term unemployment.

The Flexible New Deal will combine the New Deal 25 plus and New Deal for Young People (including private sector-led New Deals and Employment Zones). It will also replace New Deal 50 plus, the New Deal for Musicians and self-employment provision. Other voluntary programmes, such as the New Deal for Lone Parents, will continue to be available.

Phase one of the FND will begin on 5 October 2009.

The FND customers

Participants are known as customers, and are referred onto the FND after 12 months of claiming JSA.

The FND suppliers

In March 2008 the DWP advertised their FND requirements and specification, which started a lengthy tendering process. Providers, known as suppliers, then submitted Pre-Qualification Questionnaires (PPQs) before being short-listed and submitting formal tenders. Potential suppliers were encouraged to describe how they would offer an innovative, flexible, personalised and responsive service, tailored to the individual's employment and skills needs.

There will not be many main suppliers (prime contractors), and they will hold large contracts which will last five years (until October 2016). However, the DWP thinks it unlikely they will be able to deliver the FND without support from other suppliers. Therefore, subcontracting to suppliers from the private, public and third sectors is likely to be commonplace.

Jobseekers Regime and Flexible New Deal (JRFND)

The Flexible New Deal is the final stage in a four-stage JRFND process. Stages one, two and three are delivered by Jobcentre Plus, and stage four is delivered by the suppliers.

The JRFND Model

Source: *Flexible New Deal Preferred Bidder Presentation*, DWP (June 2009)

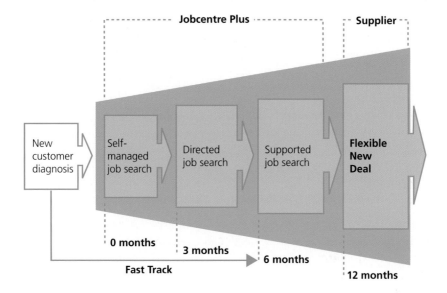

Allotted time

Customers are required to participate in the FND for 52 weeks, which is known as their FND allotted time.

Alloted time is completed once:
- a sustainable job outcome is achieved;
- 52 weeks participation is completed;
- the customer signs off JSA for 26 weeks.

During these 52 weeks every FND customer must complete at least four weeks continuous full-time employment or work-related activity. During allotted time suppliers must meet with customers at least once every fortnight for 'meaningful contact'. If the customers do not participate the supplier can raise 'sanction doubts' with Jobcentre Plus, which could result in the customer losing their benefit payments.

FND funding and rates

Funding for suppliers is split into a service fee, a short job outcome payment, and a sustained outcome payment. The service fee represents just 20 percent of the funding, and the rates for short and sustained job outcomes are determined by the contract size and performance offer within the supplier bids. Suppliers also have to work within service level tolerances.

Apprenticeships

In 1994 modern apprenticeships were introduced to raise participation and extend the original programme beyond those employment sectors with no apprenticeship tradition. The term 'modern' was dropped in 2004, and in 2009/10 there are over 180 apprenticeship frameworks on offer with funding for almost half a million learners to participate across England.

All apprenticeships are funded in 2009/10 using the demand-led formula and from the employer-responsive funding model. However, the funding comes from two government departments and is split between three age groups.

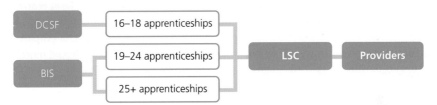

In addition, the National Apprenticeship Service (NAS) was launched in April 2009 and has accountability for the national delivery of targets, co-ordination of the funding for apprenticeship places, management of the Vacancy Matching Service (VMS), assessment of apprenticeship providers and co-ordinating and leading a national marketing and information service for employers and would-be apprentices.

Apprenticeships are available at Level 2 (apprenticeships) and 3 (advanced apprenticeships). Their frameworks are devised by the government-funded Sector Skills Councils (SSCs), which are employer-led bodies responsible for defining training requirements in their sector. Each apprenticeship works to the same blueprint, available online at www.apprenticeships.org.uk

Apprenticeship framework blueprint

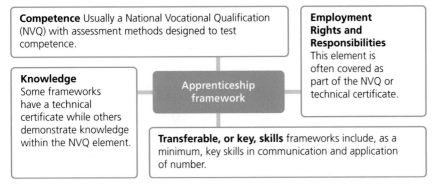

Providers must deliver learning that comprises all the elements of the relevant apprenticeship framework. This means that the framework success and associated achievement funding can only be claimed once all the elements have been successfully achieved (*see page 124*).

Apprenticeship eligibility, formula and rates

To access apprenticeship funding learners must be 16 or over at the start of the course and satisfy the LSC learner eligibility requirements (*see page 50*). There are a number of priority learner groups (such as 16–18-year-olds). Graduates, except those who have participated in the New Deal, remain ineligible for LSC apprenticeship funding. Some Sector Skills Councils impose entry requirements, so providers should refer to the relevant framework. The apprenticeship programme is primarily intended for people in employment (employer-led apprenticeship). However, a programme-led pathway will be appropriate for some young learners before employment. These can be funded under any funding model, but the LSC state: 'providers delivering programme-led pathways should actively seek employer-led apprenticeships for their learners at the earliest opportunity, and should monitor progression rates as part of quality-assurance processes'.

Funding formula

The apprenticeship funding formula works in the same way as for Train to Gain, but with the addition of the disadvantage uplift (*see page 36*).

Example funding for a main qualification in 2009/10 (excl. ALS)

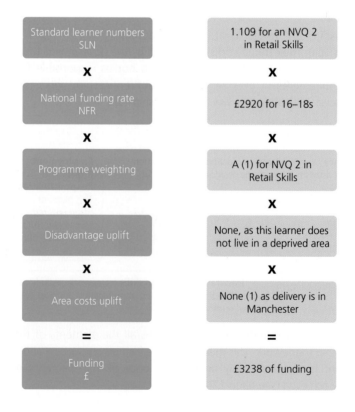

Standard learner numbers SLN	1.109 for an NVQ 2 in Retail Skills
X	**X**
National funding rate NFR	£2920 for 16–18s
X	**X**
Programme weighting	A (1) for NVQ 2 in Retail Skills
X	**X**
Disadvantage uplift	None, as this learner does not live in a deprived area
X	**X**
Area costs uplift	None (1) as delivery is in Manchester
=	**=**
Funding £	£3238 of funding

Rates

Each qualification within an apprenticeship is funded separately, and the national funding rate differs for each of the three age categories.

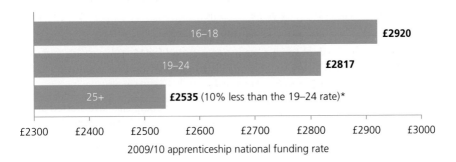

2009/10 apprenticeship national funding rate

*The actual rate used by the LSC is £2817, but this is discounted by 10% (see page 122).

In addition, all 19+ apprenticeships are co-funded, which means there is an expectation that the employer will contribute to the costs. This employer contribution (fee element) for each qualification reduces the total framework funding by approximately 47.5% (see page 122).

The table below shows the unweighted funding for a Retail Apprenticeship.

This framework (code 112) was devised by the Sector Skills Council Skillsmart Retail.

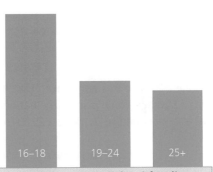

Retail Apprenticeship	SLN	2009/10 unweighted funding		
NVQ in Retail Skills (L2)	1.109	£3238	£1699	£1530
BTEC Certificate in Retailing (L2)	0.267	£780	£409	£368
Key skills in application of number (L1)	0.08	£234	£186	£167
Key skills in communication (L1)	0.08	£234	£186	£167
Total	1.536	£4485	£2480	£2232

The following pages provide further examples, and explains how the monthly on-programme and achievement instalments are calculated and paid.

16–18 apprenticeships

Learners aged 16, 17 or 18 at the start of their apprenticeship are funded from the DCSF budget. This provision is classed as a very high priority and the plan is that there will be growth for many years to come.

We want apprenticeships to be a mainstream option for 16–18-year-olds and will ensure that, by 2013, every suitably qualified young person who wants to undertake an apprenticeship is able to do so.

The ambition is that, by 2019/20, one in five young people will have started an apprenticeship before the end of the academic year in which they reach their 18th birthday (from one in 15 at present).

16–18 apprenticeships	2008/09	2009/10	Increase
Starts (academic year)	108k	116k	7%
Completions (academic year)	68k	72k	6%
Participation (academic year)	213k	223k	5%
DCSF funding (financial year)	£628m	£675m	11%

Source: *Statement of Priorities*, LSC (November 2008)

In June 2009 the LSC announced that they would make a further £70m available for 17,500 additional places. The national funding rate for 16–18 apprenticeships has also increased by 2.1% to £2920 (*see page 30*).

Apprenticeship framework funding

The following are examples of unweighted apprenticeship framework funding (SLN × £2920) for 16–18-year-olds in 2009/10.

Beauty Therapy Apprenticeship (279)	SLN	Unweighted funding
NVQ in Beauty Therapy (L2)	1.321	£3857
Key skills in application of number (L1)	0.08	£234
Key skills in communication (L1)	0.08	£234
Total framework funding	1.481	£4325

The Apprenticeship in Beauty Therapy does not have a separate technical certificate qualification. However, the blueprint remains unchanged since the knowledge is gained through delivery of the NVQ.

Some qualification rates differ between Level 2 and Level 3, which can be seen in the table below. Also, the Advanced Apprenticeship in Beauty Therapy includes key skills in ICT at Level 1.

Beauty Therapy Advanced Apprenticeship (279)	SLN	Unweighted funding
NVQ in Beauty Therapy (L3)	1.739	£5078
Key skills in application of number (L2)	0.08	£234
Key skills in communication (L2)	0.08	£234
Key skills in ICT (L1)	0.08	£5545
Total framework funding	**1.979**	**£5078**

Some frameworks include wider key skills qualifications (*see page 90*), and increasingly, functional skills are replacing key skills (*see page 91*).

Engineering Apprenticeship (106)	SLN	Unweighted funding
NVQ in Performing Engineering Operations (L2)	1.333	£3892
Certificate in Engineering (L2)	0.667	£1,948
Key skills in working with others (L2)	0.08	£234
Key skills in improving own learning and performance (L2)	0.08	£234
Functional skills mathematics (L1)	0.08	£234
Functional skills English (L1)	0.08	£234
Functional skills ICT (L1)	0.08	£234
Total framework funding	**2.4**	**£7008**

19–24 and 25+ apprenticeships

Learners aged 19 or over at the start of their apprenticeship are funded from the Department for Business, Innovation and Skills (BIS) budget.

As the table below shows, BIS are funding a 2% increase in 19+ starts for 2009/10. Funding for the financial year has increased by 12%.

19+ apprenticeships	2008/09	2009/10	Increase
Starts (academic year)	120k	122k	2%
Completions (academic year)	51k	57k	12%
Participation (academic year)	243k	254k	5%
DCSF funding (financial year)	£328m	£367m	12%

Source: *Statement of Priorities*, LSC (November 2008)

This disparity between the increase in starts and the budget has occurred in the main because of the growth in adult (25+) apprenticeships during 2008/09. Many 2008/9 starts have planned end dates after July 2009, so they will 'carry-in' their funding instalments to 2009/10 (*see page 135*).

To constrain costs, the LSC planned in November 2008 to use the extra two thousand starts in 2009/10 only for the 19–24-year-olds (making up 93k of the total 122k). However, during 2009 it became clear that the budget was in danger of being exceeded, so in June 2009 the LSC announced they would be reducing the 2009/10 25+ apprenticeship national funding rate for new starts by 10% after inflation (to make it 90% of 19–24 rate). Therefore, while the national funding rate for 19–24 apprenticeships is £2817 (1.5% more than in 2008/09) the 25+ rate is 10% lower at £2535 (*see page 30*).

Discount funding for 25+ apprenticeship starts

The reduced 25+ rate will be built directly into LSC funding software for 2010/11. However, this late policy change is 'a risk to LSC funding and payments systems', so in 2009/10 'providers are asked to discount the funding for all 25+ apprenticeship starts from 1 August using field A51a of the individualised learner record (ILR)'.

The value in field A51a of the main qualification should be '087' and for other qualifications it should be '090'. Some learners will have prior attainment, for which the A51a discount is already being used. In these cases a multiple discount should be applied. The use of the A51a field can be complex, so the latest LSC funding guidance should be consulted.

The employer contribution (fee element) percentage

All apprenticeship learners over the age of 18 at the start of their course, regardless of prior attainment, are co-funded. This means all funding is reduced by an employer contribution percentage (*see page 52*). The employer contribution percentage for each apprenticeship qualification is found in the Learning Aim Database (*see page 138*).

Level 2 Engineering Framework (106)	SLN	Fee element percentage
NVQ in Performing Engineering Operations (L2)	1.333	48.2%
Certificate in Engineering (L2)	0.667	45.6%
Key skills in working with others (L2)	0.08	17.5%
Key skills in improving own learning and performance (L2)	0.08	17.5%
Functional skills mathematics (L1)	0.08	17.5%
Functional skills English (L1)	0.08	17.5%
Functional skills ICT (L1)	0.08	17.5%

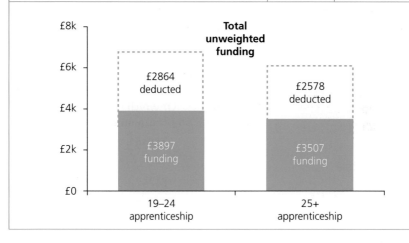

The agreed employer contributions for apprenticeships are expressed as the amount which the fully-funded 16–18 rate is reduced by to give the co-funded 19+ rate. The funding calculations and the values on the Learning Aim Database require the employer contribution to be expressed as a percentage of the 19+ rate; those percentage figures are consequently slightly lower, as the national funding rate for 19+ apprenticeships is lower than that for 16–18-year-olds. In addition, key skills have historically had a lower expected employer contribution than other learning aims and they continue to do so in 2009/10.

Source: *Funding Guidance 2009/10*, LSC (July 2009)

Monthly instalments

Apprenticeship provision, like Train to Gain, is funded in monthly on-programme instalments based on the start and planned end date with an achievement instalment in the month of the actual end date. If the learner withdraws during the course only the monthly instalments before the month in which they withdrew are paid. Conversely, if a learner achieves before the planned end date a balancing instalment ensures that the total funding is paid. If the learner fails to achieve the minimum attendance period then no funding is earned (*see page 54*).

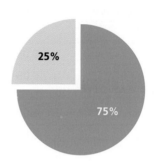

Achievement
Only paid if all qualifications in the framework are passed.

On-programme
The monthly on-programme instalments are calculated as funding divided by (months +1) with two instalments being paid in the first month to reflect higher upfront costs.

However, unlike Train to Gain, the funding split is not 75:25 for the full apprenticeship framework because the 25% achievement element only applies to the main qualification (usually an NVQ).

Retail framework for 16–18-year-olds (from example on page 119)

Retail Apprenticeship	Total funding	Of which on-programme	Of which achievement
NVQ in Retail Skills (L2)	£3238	£2429	£810
Technical certificate and key skills	£1247	£1247	£0
Total	£4485	£3676	£810

Therefore, in this example the framework funding split is 82:18.

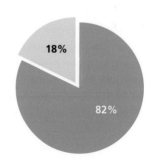

Achievement
£810 paid in the month when the framework was fully achieved.

On-programme
£3676 paid across a number of months. The (months + 1) calculation means the instalment in the first month is always twice as large as each of the remaining months.

The table below shows the monthly instalments for the 16–18-year-old learner on a Retail Apprenticeship, as described on page 119. This learner will start in September 2009 and achieve all the qualifications (the full framework) in July 2010.

Qualification	NVQ	Tech cert	Key skill	Key skill	Total
SLN	1.109	0.267	0.08	0.08	1.536
Month	Funding	Funding	Funding	Funding	**Funding**
Sep-09	£442	£142	£42	£42	£668
Oct-09	£221	£71	£21	£21	£334
Nov-09	£221	£71	£21	£21	£334
Dec-09	£221	£71	£21	£21	£334
Jan-10	£221	£71	£21	£21	£334
Feb-10	£221	£71	£21	£21	£334
Mar-10	£221	£71	£21	£21	£334
Apr-10	£221	£71	£21	£21	£334
May-10	£221	£71	£21	£21	£334
Jun-10	£221	£71	£21	£21	£334
Jul-10	£810	£0	£0	£0	£810
Total	£3238	£780	£234	£234	£4485

Carry-in learners

Apprenticeship qualification start and end dates often span more than one academic year. If a learner starts in 2008/09 and finishes in 2009/10 the instalments in 2009/10 will 'carry-in', and be calculated at 2009/10 rates. This is explained in more detail on page 135.

Profiles and payment

Every provider will have a 2009/10 maximum contract value (MCV), which will be split between 16–18, 19–24 and 25+. The MCV is profiled into monthly instalments from August 2009 to July 2010. However, the actual payments to providers are made a month in arrears on the 10th working day of the month based on data submitted on the 4th working day of the month (*see diagram on page 51*).

Note

MCVs will be monitored during the year, and they may be reduced if delivery is below profile. If delivery is above profile then MCVs can be increased, subject to affordability. However, in reality it is unlikely that providers will be able to access any further funding for 25+ apprenticeships, as the 16–18 and 19–24-year-olds are a priority.

Train to Gain

Train to Gain is officially described by the LSC as 'a brokerage service which provides impartial, independent advice on training to businesses across England'. However, the term is also used to describe a rapidly expanding training scheme funded by the LSC, which was rolled out nationally in 2006. As the graph below shows, the amount of funding allocated to Train to Gain continues to rise, and is likely to be more than £1bn by 2010.

LSC budget for Train to Gain participation

Source: *LSC Grant Letter 2009–10*, DCSF and DIUS (November 2008)

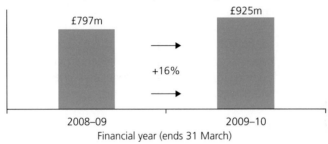

Financial year (ends 31 March)

Whilst take up of Train to Gain was initially slower than planned, the demand for funding is now outstripping supply. As a result, most providers have been given reduced or lower than anticipated 2009/10 maximum contract values (MCV). The monthly instalment profiles (August–July) have also had to be adjusted to reflect the funding available in the financial year (April–March). This problem has occurred primarily for two reasons.

1. New flexibilities

When Train to Gain funding was first introduced it was only to fund employees undertaking their first full Level 2 qualification, and a limited number of Level 1 and Level 2 basic skills qualifications. In 2008/09 this was expanded to include funding at Level 2 for learners who already have a full Level 2 qualification, full Level 3 qualifications, NVQs at Level 1 and 4 that were FE funded in 2007/08, basic skills at all levels and a limited number of unit and thin (not full Level 2 or 3) qualifications (*see page 130*).

2. The payment of monthly instalments

In 2008/09 Train to Gain funding began to be paid in monthly on-programme payments with an achievement payment at the end. This means much of the 2009/10 funding has already been committed to those that started in 2008/09 and will finish in 2009/10 (*see page 134*).

Note

The Train to Gain funding problem makes it likely that rules and approaches to contract management will change during 2009/10.

Train to Gain eligibility, formula and rates

Eligibility

To access Train to Gain funding a learner must be 19 or over at the start of the course and satisfy the LSC learner eligibility requirements (*see page 50*) as well as being one of the following:

- employed, which includes direct employment, hired from an employment business by which they are employed or seconded from another employer;
- self-employed;
- working as a volunteer.

There are complex definitions which underpin these categories and not all employers and employees are currently eligible. Providers should therefore consult the latest LSC funding guidance and regularly check their website (www.lsc.gov.uk/providers/ttg/latest) for any updates.

Funding formula

Train to Gain sits with apprenticeships within the employer-responsive funding model. Funding is calculated using a Train to Gain version of the national demand-led funding formula (*see page 27*):

Example funding for a Train to Gain enrolment in 2009/10

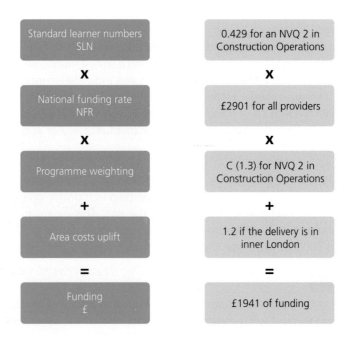

Changes to rates and programme weightings

There have been significant changes to Train to Gain rates and programme weightings for 2009/19, as outlined in the table below.

Change type	2008/09 value	2009/10 value
SLN value for full Level 2 or below	0.429 higher rate	0.429 (occasionally 0.493)
	0.286 lower rate	
SLN value for full Level 3 or above	0.644 higher rate	0.644
	0.429 lower rate	
SLN value for Skills for Life (literacy, numeracy and ESOL)	0.18	0.193
National funding rate (increased by 1.5%)	£2858 (including the 3% additional uplift)	£2901 (3% additional uplift scrapped)
Top programme weighting (excluding Skills for Life)	K (1.5)	C (1.3)
Middle programme weighting	J (1.25)	L (1.2) and reducing to 1.15 in 2010/11
Skills for Life programme weighting	K (1.5)	F (1.4)

The 2009/10 SLN values and programme weightings in the table above are 'typical'. The Learning Aim Database (LAD) should be consulted for the relevant qualification to establish the correct Train to Gain SLN and programme weighting (*see page 138*). Checking the LAD will be particularly important as new qualifications become eligible for Train to Gain under the QCF interim definitions of full Level 2 and full Level 3 (*see page 22*).

Supplementary information about Train to Gain:
- If learners are ineligible for fee remission, the 2009/10 fee element (funding amount deducted) is 47.5% of the total funding.
- Funding is paid in monthly instalments (75% for on-programme payments and 25% for achievement) (*see page 134*).
- Information is available in the 2009/10 LSC funding guidance for providers who want to use workbooks and distance learning.

Train to Gain flexibilities

The Government introduced additional funding flexibilities for 2008/09 to stimulate demand for Train to Gain provision. Further flexibilities were then announced at the end of October 2008 in response to the economic downturn. These significant enhancements were intended to drive up volumes and spend, and they have proved so successful that demand has already outstripped the supply of funding. As a result, a number of flexibilities have already been removed. Further changes are anticipated during 2009/10 so providers should visit www.lsc.gov.uk/providers/ttg/latest for updates.

Original flexibility	Status for 2009/10 as at August 2009
New high funding rate threshold	The high and low funding rates have been replaced in 2009/10 with a single rate for each enrolment.
Increasing the rates by an additional 3% each year	The LSC announced in June 2009 that they would be scrapping this additional 3% as it was unaffordable.
Numeracy and literacy eligible at any level	No change. Full literacy and numeracy qualifications at Entry Level 1–3, Level 1 and Level 2 will be fully funded for learners irrespective of prior attainment. However, the expectation is that the majority of enrolments will be at Entry 3 and above (target-bearing).
ESOL eligible at any level	No change. Full ESOL qualifications at any level (including the ESOL for Work qualification) are eligible for Train to Gain co-funding (47.5% reduction).
NVQ Level 1	This was a temporary flexibility for colleges delivering FE-funded NVQ Level 1 qualifications in the workplace during 2007/08. Only learners finishing their programme during 2009/10 will be funded.
Additional Level 2s permitted	No change. A limited relaxation on firstness will be permitted for qualifications on the agreed list (see LSC website).
All Level 2s fully funded	No change. All Level 2 Train to Gain qualifications will be fully funded.

Original flexibility	Status for 2009/10 as at August 2009
Additional Level 3s	No change. A limited relaxation on firstness will be permitted for qualifications on the agreed list.
19–25 first full Level 3 entitlement	No change. The 19–25 entitlement has been extended to Train to Gain, which means learners under 25 years of age at the start of the course who do not have a first full Level 3 will be fully funded. Also, any learner of any age who does not already possess the equivalent of a first full Level 2 would be fully funded at Level 3 (Level 3 jumpers). All other Level 3 learners would remain co-funded (47.5% reduction in funding).
Level 4/5	This was a temporary flexibility for colleges delivering FE-funded NVQ Level 4 and 5 qualifications in the workplace during 2007/08. Only learners finishing the programme during 2009/10 will be funded. The qualifications must also be on the 'agreed list'. If a learner does not already posses a full Level 2 qualification or is eligible for the 19–25 entitlement the NVQ 4 would be fully funded.
Units and thin qualifications	The list of QCF units and thin (less than full) qualifications that were published in December 2008 remains available to providers (*see page 132*). However, it is no longer permissible for a learner to undertake them concurrently with a Level 2, Level 3 or Skills for Life qualification.

Potential changes to flexibilities

As previously mentioned, the existing flexibilities have led to the demand for funding exceeding supply. It is therefore likely that many of the flexibilities that remain for 2009/10 will either be changed or removed. For example, when the Skills Funding Agency (SFA) take over responsibility for funding Train to Gain provision from April 2010 they may decide it is no longer affordable to fully fund all Level 2 learners. They may also want to prioritise Train to Gain funding for those who have recently entered employment. For example, the LSC-funded Six-month Offer programme includes a bonus payment for learners progressing onto Train to Gain programmes (*see page 112*).

Providers should expect the flexibilities to be scaled back, and be mindful to prioritise those employees who would benefit most from the training.

Unitised and thin qualifications

In response to the issues facing small and medium-sized enterprises (SMEs) during the economic downturn, the Government announced in October 2008 a Train to Gain SME offer. This SME offer included funding for a limited range of units and thin qualifications from January 2009.

Employer eligibility

SMEs are defined as an enterprise with less than 250 full-time equivalent employees (FTEs). One FTE is a minimum of 35 hours per week and anyone who works part-time, seasonally or for part of a year, should be treated as a fraction of one FTE. The latest LSC guidance should be consulted to confirm eligible and ineligible organisations.

Employers are required to confirm the number of FTE employees within their organisation and thereby agree eligibility by completing an appropriate auditable declaration.

Unit and thin qualification types

The list of eligible QCF units and thin qualifications selected for the SME offer were chosen to support the following business-critical areas:
- business improvement, including business systems and processes
- customer service, including communications
- new product design
- IT pro specialist function where IT is at the heart of the business
- management, including risk management and team working
- marketing and sales
- risk management
- SME finance (including finance, credit, cashflow and profit management)

A list of the units and thin qualifications reside on the LSC website, and the intention is that they will be updated regularly in response to identified employer need (see *www.traintogain.gov.uk*).

Funding units and thin qualifications

The funding for units and thin qualifications use the same funding formula as for all Train to Gain qualifications:

$$SLN \times NFR \times PW \times ACU = \text{Train to Gain funding}$$

All SLN values for Train to Gain units and thin qualifications have been assigned one of six funding bands. A higher proportion of the overall cost relating to administration, registration and assessment has been taken into account in setting the SLN value. The SLN values are held for each unit and qualification within the Learning Aim Database (*see page 138*).

Funding band	SLN	2009/10 unweighted funding
1	0.028	£81
2	0.054	£157
3	0.079	£229
4	0.101	£293
5	0.126	£366
6	0.15	£435

A mix of eligible units and thin qualifications up to a maximum total value of 15 funding bands can be undertaken by an individual in a 12-month period, and there are no rules of combination specific to eligible units. The table below contains an example programme with the maximum of 15 bands.

Eligible enrolment	Level	Band	SLN	2009/10 unweighted funding
IT consulting skills (unit)	3	5	0.126	£366
Planning in business (unit)	2	1	0.028	£81
Award in leadership (thin qualification)	4	3	0.079	£229
Award in business finance (thin qualification)	3	6	0.15	£435
Total		15	0.383	£1111

The fee eligibility criteria is applied in the same way for unit and thin qualifications as for full qualifications.

The LSC are also using this offer as a vehicle for testing out approaches to unit funding and the broader QCF trials within the employer-responsive funding model (*see page 22*). This means that:

- progression on to full Level 2 and 3 qualifications is encouraged and will be monitored;

- when a learner progresses from an individual unit or thin qualification onto a full qualification which contains the same content, the relevant funding should be discounted using field A51a in the ILR.

Monthly instalments

Train to Gain qualifications, like apprenticeships, are funded in monthly on-programme instalments based on the start and planned end date with an achievement instalment in the month of the actual end date. If the learner withdraws during the course only the monthly instalments before the month in which they withdrew are paid. Conversely, if a learner achieves before the planned end date a balancing instalment ensures that the total funding is paid. If the learner fails to achieve the minimum attendance period then no funding is earned (*see page 54*).

Achievement

25%

75%

On-programme

The monthly on-programme instalments are calculated as funding divided by (months +1) with two instalments being paid in the first month to reflect higher upfront costs.

The graph below shows funding instalments for a Train to Gain qualification with a total weighted funding of £1618.

October instalment £485	November instalment £243	December instalment £243	January instalment £243	February achievement £404

£0   £200   £400   £600   £1000   £1200   £1400   £1600

Using the example above, the table below shows how much funding would be earned in these months if one learner started per month.

	October	November	December	January	February
Learner A	£485	£243	£243	£243	£404
Learner B	£0	£485	£243	£243	£243
Learner C	£0	£0	£485	£243	£243
Learner D	£0	£0	£0	£485	£243
Learner E	£0	£0	£0	£0	£485
Total	£485	£728	£971	£1213	£1618

Monthly instalments make cash-flow planning complex as the funding profile is dependent on both the start and end dates. It can also lead to larger than expected total monthly payments in future months and years.

Carry-in learners

A full Level 2 qualification delivered through Train to Gain usually takes six months or more to deliver. This means learners starting their course in the middle of one academic year will not achieve until some time in the next year. These enrolments in their second year are referred to as 'carry-in', since they started in a previous year. The on-programme and achievement instalments in the second year of a course are funded at the new rates.

The table below shows the rates and funding for an NVQ in Construction at the lower SLN rate in 2008/09 and in 2009/10 (when there is just one rate).

Year	Qualification	SLN	NFR	PW	Funding
2008/09	NVQ in Construction	0.286	£2858	1.5	£1226
2009/10	NVQ in Construction	0.429	£2901	1.3	£1618

If a learner were to start in May in the 2008/09 academic year and carry-in to October in the 2009/10 academic year the funding would be £1421. This is because half the instalments would be at 2008/09 rates and half would be at 2009/10 rates, as shown in the graph below.

Profiles and payment

Every provider will have a 2009/10 maximum contract value (MCV) which is profiled into monthly instalments from August 2009 to July 2010. However, the actual payments to providers are made a month in arrears on the 10th working day of the month based on data submitted on the 4th working day of the month (*see diagram on page 51*).

This payment system is creating a considerable problem for the LSC as their budgets are based on the financial year (April–March) rather than the academic year (August–July). In London, for example, only 47% of the academic year funding is available to spend in the financial year ending March 2009. This means providers can only be paid up to 47% of their MCV for the first eight months (67%) of the academic year.

Hints and tips

The hints and tips chapter briefly covers some other funding-related topics and provides additional information which may prove useful.

Learning Aim Database

The Learning Aim Database (LAD) is the definitive source of information concerning the funding eligibility, rate, and programme weighting for every qualification or programme of learning. If providers want to know the funding for a course, the first place to look is on the LAD. This section also explains the importance of learning aims and how to search for them and related information on the LAD.

Funding optimisation

Funding optimisation is a widely used term that covers activities designed to increase funding relative to cost. At the extreme this is a questionable practice which exploits the principals, rules, and spirit of the funding guidance. However, when planning efficient and cost-effective provision there remain important things to consider. This section focuses on five of these as well as the LSC's *Principles of Funding Learning*.

Target setting

Targets are an increasingly important part of the funding relationship between the LSC and providers. They come in a variety of types such as funding, SLN, learner, week, starts and success rates. They are used at different times and in different ways within different funding models, and can also be catagorised into priority and non-priority provision. This section takes a closer look at the targets and the ways to record them.

Performance monitoring

Once targets have been set, the way they are monitored and reported is important. This monitoring can ensure interventions address performance issues before targets are missed. It is also important to the funding agency as they use performance reports to alter maximum contracts or as the basis for determining negotiated or tendered funding. This section takes a close look at the new post-16 performance assessment framework called Framework for Excellence.

Decimal-led funding

When calculating learner-responsive funding the number of decimal places used for the SLN and provider factor determines the exact amount of funding. Not knowing the number of decimal places used may, in reality, not be a significant problem. However, this section explains why unknown decimals may be the reason providers doing their own calculations cannot match the official funding reports.

Beyond 2009/10

There will be significant changes during 2009/10, as from April 2010 the LSC ceases to exist. In addition, there are a number of significant longer-term reforms which providers should be keeping a close eye on. This section takes a brief look at these in terms of what is in the pipeline for the post-16 education and training sector.

The Learning Aim Database

Providers should know their way around the Learning Aim Database (LAD) because it is the definitive source of funding and statistical information for LSC-recognised learning aims.

The LAD holds data for three teaching years (currently 2007/08, 2008/09 and 2009/10) and can be searched online or downloaded as a database from the web address below.

> **http://providers.lsc.gov.uk/lad**

The collection of information within the LAD is the responsibility of the Data Service (www.thedataservice.org.uk), who add and amend aims each month based on details received from a variety of sources, including DCSF, BIS, QCDA, Ofqual, awarding bodies and providers.

Learning aims

Every enrolment within an individualised learner record (ILR) must have one eight-digit learning aim (also sometimes referred to as the QCA or Ofqual reference). Most learning aims are unique to the qualification title, level and awarding body. Once the correct learning aim has been found on the LAD, a series of tabs guide the user to the relevant information. The table on the following page shows just some of the information available.

Searching the LAD

The LAD search engine can be very useful. For example, key words can be used to search for a particular qualification or for all qualifications at a particular level in a particular sector subject area. Once the relevant learning aim has been found there is often a link to the National Database of Accredited Qualification (NDAQ) at www.accreditedqualifications.org.uk which contains even more information about the qualification (such as the unit structure). This makes the LAD a powerful tool, not only for determining rates, but for finding out about the availability of qualifications.

Generic learning aims

In some cases, such as for non-certificated provision or for units of qualifications, a generic learning aim is required. Details of how to use generic learning aims can be found within Annex H of the ILR specification, available from the Information Authority (www.theia.org.uk). Below is an example of a generic learning aim, and how it is made up:

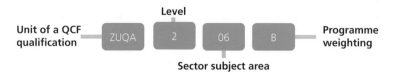

Selection of information for a qualification held on the LAD	
Learning Aim reference	10055848
Learning Aim title	NVQ in Construction Operations
Level	2
Awarding body	Edexcel
Learner-responsive SLN glh	520
Learner-responsive programme weighting	D (1.6)
Apprenticeship SLN	1.064
Apprenticeship employer contribution	45.6%
Apprenticeship programme weighting	K (1.5)
Apprenticeship framework	The LAD includes functionality to view all the relevant qualifications within a framework
Train to Gain SLN	0.429
Train to Gain programme weighting	C (1.3)
Whether or not a qualification contributes to a PSA target	This is a full Level 2 qualification
Number of Qualifications and Credit Framework (QCF) credits	This qualification is not on the QCF
The sector subject area	Construction, Planning and the Built Environment
Whether it is fundable, and for which funding model	This includes the relevant accreditation and certificate end dates

Funding optimisation

The term funding optimisation is popular with some providers and consultants. However, the aim should always be to ensure sufficient funding is generated to deliver a high-quality service, rather than simply raising the average funding per learner. There are perhaps five critical and responsible things that providers should focus on to ensure sufficient and efficient funding is generated:

1. Check and monitor the learning aims
Learning aims determine funding eligibility, the funding value (SLN glh) and programme weightings. They should be annually audited for accuracy and monitored, as their status and rates can change (*see page 138*).

2. Set appropriate course sizes
The course size in terms of guided learning hours (glh) will not only be important to the learner, it will be the key determinant of cost. Therefore, as funding values are described in terms of SLN glh, providers should check that their own glh does not vary wildly from LSC's SLN glh. Also, providers should check that funded programme size does not unknowingly exceed the annual 1.75 SLN (787.5 SLN glh). Of course, providers are free to set durations below or above LSC rates.

3. Recruit and retain sufficient group sizes
It is important to remember that demand-led funding is an enrolment-based funding methodology. In other words, while the cost per group will depend on the size and duration, the revenue is heavily dependant on the number of enrolments. Therefore in terms of 16–18 and adult learner-responsive funding, perhaps the most critical aspect of optimisation is class size. The funding rates are based on an expectation that there will be approximately 14 learners in a class. So as a rule of thumb, if class sizes are less than 14 the course will be running at a loss. Put another way, the most efficient providers are likely to have the larger classes (assuming quality does not suffer). Therefore, achieving appropriate class sizes is very important. This makes the monitoring of recruitment important, as will being able and willing to switch resources quickly to those courses with sufficient demand.

4. Maintain high success rates
Providers with high success rates will benefit from a high success factor (*see page 42*). So funding can be optimised by ensuring learners achieve.

5. Regularly check the validity of the data
The individualised learner record (ILR) is the data which generates funding. If the ILR is incorrect, then it is highly likely the funding will also be incorrect. The LSC publish a data self-assessment toolkit (DSAT) which providers are expected to use to regularly check the validity of their ILR data (particularly in terms of some of the eligibility criteria).

Keep it in the spirit of the guidance

The LSC have not created a funding rule for every circumstance, and therefore 'it is expected that providers will fully comply with the spirit and intention of the funding principles'. This spirit is described in the LSC *2008/09 Principles Rules and Regulations* funding guidance booklet. In potential conflict with optimisation, it makes it clear that when planning provision, *funding should not heavily outweigh cost.*

Principles of funding learning

The funding provided to schools, colleges and other providers should reflect the directly incurred costs of efficiently delivered provision (with an appropriate contribution to overheads) within the national funding framework and rates.

All LSC funded providers should:

- claim funding at national rates to reflect the costs of delivery and ensure that multiple funding for provision is not claimed. Providers should use ILR field A51a to discount funding in cases where too much funding would otherwise be claimed;

- ensure that duplication of provision in a learner's programme of study is avoided and, where this occurs because of an overlap in learning aim content, adjust the funding claimed to reflect the degree of overlap;

- consider guided learning hours (glh) as the key driver of costs incurred when determining the level of funding claimed in 16–18 and adult learner-responsive funding systems;

- consider costs of delivering provision and assessment in the workplace (together with any associated glh) as the key driver of costs incurred when determining the level of funding claimed via the employer-responsive funding model;

- discuss with the relevant funding agency what funding should be claimed in circumstances where the calculation of funding to be claimed results in a level of funding that is clearly well in excess of the costs incurred;

- discuss with the relevant funding agency what funding should be claimed where providers wish to deliver provision that is in the best interests of their learners but the funding arrangement is viewed as a barrier;

- avoid claiming LSC funding for any part of any learner's programme of study that duplicates what is received from any other source, for example a different LSC funding stream, their employer or the Higher Education Funding Council for England (HEFCE).

Target setting

Targets are clearly important, and to a great extent providers will succeed or fail according to their skill at setting and achieving appropriate targets. Targets have become increasingly important for a number of reasons.

- Government funding is increasingly being targeted at those providers delivering high-quality priority provision.
- Public Service Agreement (PSA) targets have been stretched and are increasingly determining which provision receives funding.
- Reconciliation to adult learner-responsive funding will be on the basis of in-year and year end priority SLN targets (*see page 95*).
- Employer-responsive funding will only be earned once delivered.

Targets in the post-16 sector come in a variety of forms and are used at different times and in different ways within different funding models. They are also increasingly being split between priority and non-priority provision. For example, targets can be in the form of funding, SLNs, FTEs, learner participation, starts, weeks, retention, achievement, and/or success.

In the context of the LSC, many targets reside within the summary statement of activity (SSoA). The SSoA was introduced by the LSC in 2007/08, and is a numerical summary of provision the LSC funds. It contains a complex and detailed range of funding, learner participation and SLN figures for three funding models, along with other targets such as full-cost income.

Note

The SSoA is a national template with national counting methodologies, both of which are available online. However, some regional LSCs have adopted either different or additional approaches to targets and the SSoA. It is therefore advisable for providers to consider both the national and regional arrangements when it comes to target setting.

Hints and tips for target setting

- Always be clear about the difference between an enrolment and a learner target. This is particularly important where a learner is enrolled for two PSA target-bearing qualifications (such as literacy and an NVQ Level 2). The learner target is one, yet the PSA sub-targets added together equal two. Therefore, at qualification level in a template such as the SSoA there should be an expectation that the priority sub-targets will sometimes exceed the total learner target.
- Always use the Learning Aim Database (LAD) to determine which qualifications do and do not contribute to PSA targets (*see page 138*).

- Participation targets include all learners who are on-programme during the given year. This means that learners who have a start and end date in more than one academic year become 'carry-in' learners for the second year. These learners are effectively counted twice, as they count towards the participation target in the first year, and will count towards the participation target in the following year. Providers need to be aware of 'carry-in' learners as they will generate only a proportion of the total funding in the year in question. In terms of a sales (new business) target it is therefore advisable to separate 'carry-in' from new starts (particularly within the employer-responsive funding model).
- Many providers plan at learner group level with target class sizes. The different rates within each funding model makes the setting of sub-targets for mixed cohorts vital when planning provision.

A college may set targets and calculate funding as follows:

Pretend College group (*see page 46*)	Target	of which (sub-targets)		
		16–18	19+ fully remitted	19+ co-funded
Learners in the group	18	10	6	2
SLN per learner	1.2	1.2	1.2	1.2
Total SLN	21.6	12	7.2	2.4
Funding rate	n/a	£2920	£2817	£1938
Provider factor	n/a	1.419	1.523	1.523
LSC funding total	£87,697	£49,722	£30,890	£7085

This group is therefore contributing £49,722 towards the 16–18 model allocation and £37,975 towards the adult learner-responsive allocation.

Setting sub-targets in this way also means that the provider factor can be altered at course level (such as by incorporating the actual programme weighting rather than the average figure used in the provider factor) to help set more reliable departmental or cost-centre funding targets.

Note

Learners who do not generate any funding will not contribute towards a target. Therefore, providers should consider the impact that the minimum attendance period has on their recruitment targets. See page 54 for more information about the minimum attendance period.

Performance monitoring

Once provision has been planned, and funding targets have been set, it is then important to monitor performance during the year and at its end.

Funding performance
The learner information suite (LIS) is the LSC software which calculates provider funding based on the individualised learner record (ILR) and Learning Aim Database (LAD). The LIS contains a series of useful reports, and a database can be exported which contains all the derived data.

Success rates
The Data Service is responsible for the production of post-16 data and success rates (percentage of those who start that achieve), and it maintains a data dictionary which 'is a central repository of information about business and data related terms used by the LSC' (www.thedataservice.org.uk). The success rate methodologies differ between schools and colleges, and the college success rate calculation used by Ofsted has now changed to reflect demand-led funding. Quarterly qualification success rate (QSR) reports are produced for Train to Gain and apprenticeship provision. For employer-responsive provision it is important to understand the difference between overall and timely success. Providers can access their success rate reports from the LSC provider gateway (https://gateway.lsc.gov.uk).

Minimum levels of performance
Minimum levels of performance (MLP) reports were introduced in 2006 and contain weighted success rates with various performance thresholds for provision by duration, level and sector. If insufficient provision is above the threshold a provider is served with a formal notice to improve (NTI). If the following year the provision remains below the threshold, the LSC could choose to stop funding the poorly-performing provision. This might result in the LSC seeking an alternative provider via open competitive tendering.

Programme/qualification type	2008/09 MLP	2009/10 MLP
FE long qualifications (below Level 4 and excluding A-levels)	55%	60%
A-levels	75%	75%
FE long qualifications Level 4 or higher	55%	58%
FE short qualifications (all levels)	62%	62%
Apprenticeships (full framework)	45%	50%
Train to Gain	65%	65%

Framework for excellence

The framework for excellence (FfE) is the Government's performance assessment framework for further education colleges, post-16 education and training providers currently funded by the LSC. It was piloted in 2008 and for 2009 the framework has been made much simpler. It will apply to colleges and training providers in 2009, and to school sixth forms (subject to further developments and evaluation) from 2010. The framework will also support the piloting of the school report card.

The FfE consists of core (applied to all providers) and specific (applied only to relevant providers) indicators. Each indicator is calculated to establish a grade, and some of the grades will be published. At present, the intention is not to produce an overall performance rating.

Framework for excellence performance indicators for 2009/10

Source: *Framework for Excellence: Unified Post-16 Performance Assessment*, LSC (July 2009)

Catagory	Indicator	Core or specific	Published or unpublished
Learner and qualification success	Qualification success rates	Core	Published
Learner views	Learner views	Core	Published
Learner destinations	Learner destinations	Core	Published
Responsiveness to employers	Employer views	Specific	Published
	Amount of training (not graded)	Specific	Published
	Training quality standard (TQS)	Specific	Published
Financial health and management	Financial health	Specific	Unpublished
	Financial management and control evaluation	Specific	Unpublished
Resource efficiency	Cost per successful outcome	Core	Unpublished

Framework for Excellence grades will be used by:
- **providers** – for review, self-assessment and self-evaluation;
- **commissioners and funders** – to inform, support and determine funding decisions as part of new national commissioning frameworks;
- **learners and employers** – to help them make choices.

Decimal-led funding

The demand-led national funding formula is significantly different from that which came before, not least because standard learner numbers (SLNs) come with decimal places. In the 16–18 and adult learner-responsive model the LSC do not actually publish the SLNs, they publish the SLN in terms of guided learning hours (SLN glh). The SLN glh is then converted into an SLN by dividing it by 450 (see page 30).

For example, an AS qualification taught during the day has a listed value of 150 SLN glh, which is then divided by 450 to determine the SLN value. Is this SLN value 0.3, 0.33, 0.333 or 0.3333? All these answers are of course correct, as an AS-level is worth one third of one SLN, which is 0.3 SLN recurring. The number of decimal places used for the SLN will impact on the total funding. For example, with a £2920 funding rate, 0.3 SLN generates £876, while 0.3333 SLN generates £973.

SLN decimal places can make a significant difference, as shown below.

Example of unweighted funding for AS qualifications

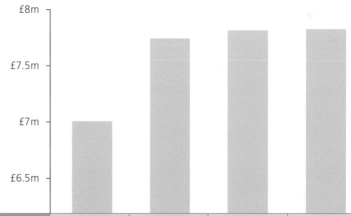

150 SLN glh	1 decimal	2 decimal	3 decimal	4 decimal
150 / 450 =	0.3	0.33	0.333	0.3333
Learners	2000	2000	2000	2000
AS per learner	4	4	4	4
Total SLN	2400	2640	2664	2666
Funding rate	£2920	£2920	£2920	£2920
Funding	£7,008,000	£7,708,800	£7,778,880	£7,785,888
Increase beyond 1 decimal		£700,800	£770,880	£777,888

There are many qualifications where this presents a problem, another of which is the full-time NVQ. This is listed at 520 SLN glh. Once divided by 450 this is 1.1555555555555555555555555555555555555555r SLN.

In the example shown in the graph below, every additional decimal place for a full-time NVQ SLN reduces funding.

Example of unweighted funding for full-time NVQ qualifications

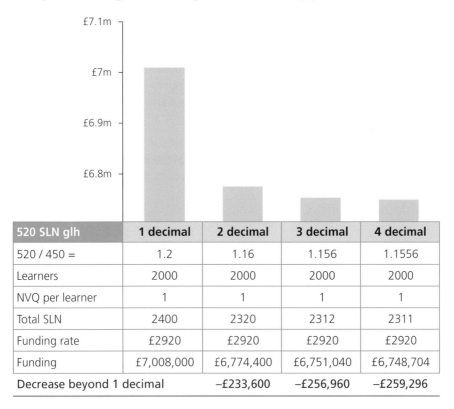

520 SLN glh	1 decimal	2 decimal	3 decimal	4 decimal
520 / 450 =	1.2	1.16	1.156	1.1556
Learners	2000	2000	2000	2000
NVQ per learner	1	1	1	1
Total SLN	2400	2320	2312	2311
Funding rate	£2920	£2920	£2920	£2920
Funding	£7,008,000	£6,774,400	£6,751,040	£6,748,704
Decrease beyond 1 decimal		−£233,600	−£256,960	−£259,296

The same problem occurs with the elements within, and calculation for, the provider factor (see page 32). These are published for each provider by the LSC to three or four decimal places, but in reality they will run to many more.

To be fair, beyond three decimal places the impact is small and the LSC software will use many more, but this does raise two important points.
1. When planning provision, use at least three decimal places for SLNs.
2. Decimal places may be the reason you cannot agree the total in an LSC funding calculation. You may get close, but it is unlikely the pounds and/or pence will be the same unless the full SLN and provider factor (with decimal places) match in both calculations.

Beyond 2009/10

There are a number of important reforms which will have a significant impact on post-16 funding during and beyond 2009/10. This section summarises a number of these, although a general election in 2010, regardless of which party wins, will inevitably lead to many new policies, as well as amendments to existing ones.

Curriculum reform

The introduction of the Diplomas in 2008/09 represented the start of some very significant reforms to 14–19 and adult qualifications.

- In March 2008 the DCSF launched the consultation *Promoting achievement, valuing success: a strategy for 14–19 qualification*. This led to the creation of a Joint Advisory Committee for Qualifications Approval (JACQA) and a vision for 2013 to have 'a streamlined credit-based system based on four nationally-available qualification suites or frameworks'.

- UK Vocational Qualification Reform Programme (UKVQRP) is being led by the sector skills councils to make qualifications QCF-compatible. This will enable LSC to 'align public funding to priority qualifications' for 2010/11 (*see page 22*).

Legislative reform

The *Education and Skills Bill 2007* raised the compulsory age of participation in education or training to 17-year-olds by 2013, and 18-year-olds by 2015. The *Apprenticeships, Children, Skills and Learning Bill 2008–09* was introduced into the House of Commons in February 2009. It was still going through committee stages in the House of Lords during October, at which time the main proposals were as follows.

- **Apprenticeships**: All suitably qualified young people would be entitled to an apprenticeship place.

- **Right to request time to train**: All employees will be given a right to request from their employer time away from their core duties to undertake training.

- **Reforms to delivery of post-16 education and training**: see following page.

- **Young offender learning**: Responsibility for securing education for young people in juvenile custody will be placed with local authorities.

- **Sixth form colleges**: A separate legal definition will be given to sixth form colleges to give them a closer relationship with their home local authority.

- **Establishment of QCDA and Ofqual**: The QCA will evolve into the QCDA and the Bill will provide for the set-up of Ofqual (the new regulator of qualifications, exams and tests in England) on a formal basis, equipping it with new powers.

Structural reform

From April 2010 the LSC will cease to exist and all 16–18 learner-responsive funding will be channelled through two new agencies. The Young People's Learning Agency (YPLA) will fund and support local authorities, who have formed 43 sub-regional groupings (SRGs) with regional planning groups (RPGs). Each local authority will then fund 16–18 schools and colleges based on a new national commissioning framework. The Skills Funding Agency (SFA) will take strategic direction from the Regional Development Agencies (RDAs), and fund adult learner-repsonsive and employer-responsive provision. The SFA will house the new National Apprenticeships Service (NAS) and the Adult Advancement and Careers Service (AACS).

Key agencies involved in funding from April 2010

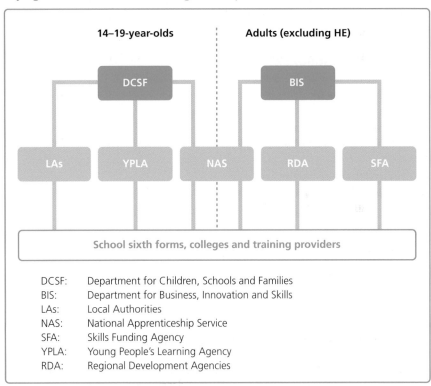

DCSF:	Department for Children, Schools and Families
BIS:	Department for Business, Innovation and Skills
LAs:	Local Authorities
NAS:	National Apprenticeship Service
SFA:	Skills Funding Agency
YPLA:	Young People's Learning Agency
RDA:	Regional Development Agencies

New White Paper

It is widely anticipated that BIS will publish a skills activism White Paper in November 2009. This is likely, amongst other things, to clarify the role for RDAs in the structure above. Other reforms likely to feature include the future of skills accounts (*see page 19*), new commissioning arrangements, and a series of reforms that would generally support industrial strategies designed to enable the economy to recover from the recession in a speedy and sustainable manner.

Web resources

The following are useful websites that contain information about post-16 funding, data and qualifications. To download documents referred to within this guide visit the official website at www.fundingguide.co.uk

LSC website

www.lsc.gov.uk
The Learning and Skills Council homepage
http://research.lsc.gov.uk/
The homepage for LSC research
http://pam.lsc.gov.uk/
The Planning and Modelling System (PaMS) homepage
https://thegateway.lsc.gov.uk
Provider Gateway, for document exchange and access to PaMS
http://ffe.lsc.gov.uk/
The LSC Framework for Excellence homepage
http://providers.lsc.gov.uk/
Provider extranet for Online Data Collection Portal and LAD
http://e2e.lsc.gov.uk
The Entry to Employment homepage
https://lsc.bravosolution.co.uk
The Learning and Skills eTendering Portal

Qualification websites

www.edexcel.com/quals
Edexcel's suite of qualifications
www.qcda.gov.uk
The Qualifications and Curriculum Development Agency (QCDA)
www.qcda.gov.uk/5396.aspx
The QCDA website for the 14–19 Diploma
www.ofqual.gov.uk/
The Office of the Qualifications and Examinations Regulator
www.accreditedqualifications.org.uk
The National Database of Accredited Qualifications
www.apprenticeships.org.uk
The apprenticeship website, containing all the frameworks
http://www.dcsf.gov.uk/section96
The Government website for qualifications for those under 19 years of age
http://www.dcsf.gov.uk/section97
The Government website for qualifications for those over 18 years of age
http://qfr.lsc.gov.uk/
The LSC's Qualification and Framework Reform homepage
http://providers.lsc.gov.uk/LAD/
The LSC's Learning Aim Database (downloads and search engine)

Government websites

www.bis.gov.uk
The Department for Business, Innovation and Skills
www.dcsf.gov.uk
The Department for Children, Schools and Families
www.dwp.gov.uk/
The Department for Work and Pensions
www.traintogain.gov.uk
The official Train to Gain website

Data websites

www.thedataservice.org.uk
The Data Service, who are responsible for data collection dissemination
www.theia.org.uk
The Information Authority, who publish the ILR specification
www.miap.gov.uk
Managing Information Across Partners, who handle the sharing of data
www.lsc.gov.uk/Providers/Data
The area on the LSC website for data news and software downloads
www.jisc.ac.uk
The Joint Information Systems Committee homepage

Other agencies

www.ukces.org.uk
The UK Commission for Employment and Skills
www.sscalliance.org
The Alliance of Sector Skills Councils
www.ofsted.gov.uk
The Office for Standards in Education
www.apprenticeships.org.uk
National Apprenticeship Service

Selection of websites with useful and free resources

www.fundingguide.co.uk
The official homepage for this practical guide to funding
www.edexcel.com/policies
Sign up to receive or download Edexcel's *Policy Watch* papers
www.aoc.co.uk
The Association of Colleges
www.learningproviders.org.uk
The Association of Learning Providers
www.lsneducation.org.uk
The Learning and Skills Network
www.niace.org.uk
The National Institute of Adult Continuing Education

Notes

You can use this section to fill in your own funding formula figures.

School sixth form provider factor elements (*see page 32*)	
Programme weighting	
Disadvantage uplift	
Area costs uplift	
Short-programme modifier	
Success factor	

Provider factor

School sixth form allocation elements (*see page 27*)	
Standard learner numbers (SLN)	
National or transitional funding rate (FR)	
Additional learning support (ALS)	

School sixth form	SLN	×	FR	×	PF	+	ALS
Funding formula							

2009/10 allocation

College provider factor	16–18	Adult
Programme weighting		
Disadvantage uplift		
Area costs uplift		
Short-programme modifier		
Success factor		

Provider factor

College allocation elements	16–18	Adult
Standard learner numbers (SLN)		
National or transitional funding rate (FR)		
Co-funded funding rate (see page 52)	N/A	
Additional learning support (ALS)		

16–18 college	SLN	×	FR	×	PF	+	ALS
Funding formula							

2009/10 allocation

Adult college	SLN	×	FR	×	PF	+	ALS
Fully-funded							
Co-funded							

2009/10 Allocation